Mediterranean Diet Made Easy

© Copyright 2023 by Thelma Ansen

TABLE OF CONTENTS

Dedicated to all my friends and to all the people
who gave me their help.
Thanks a lot
Thanks to all of you for your confidence
in my qualities and what I do.
Thelma Ansen

INTRODUCTION

Understanding the Mediterranean Diet

The Mediterranean diet conjures visions of azure coastlines, brightly colored produce, and relaxed conviviality. But this way of eating is about more than ambiance. Centered around whole, minimally processed foods like vegetables, fruits, legumes, grains, herbs, nuts, healthy fats, and seafood, the Mediterranean diet offers scientifically-proven health benefits for the body and mind. As we explore the origins, principles, and advantages of this approach, you will gain essential knowledge to start transitioning to a Mediterranean lifestyle.

The Mediterranean diet was inspired by the traditional cuisines of countries surrounding the Mediterranean Sea, including Spain, France, Italy, Greece, and parts of the Middle East. While diverse, these cuisines share certain characteristics - abundant plant foods, freshness, and simplicity. Meals celebrate high quality ingredients at their seasonal peak. Local, flavorful extra virgin olive oil forms the cornerstone, along with legumes, yogurt, nuts, whole grains, herbs, spices, and seafood. While meat and poultry play a supporting role, the meat of choice is often lamb or goat. Desserts typically involve fruits, nuts, or yogurt rather than refined sugar. Wine is enjoyed in moderation with meals. Mealtimes provide an opportunity for leisurely socializing with family and friends.

At its core, the Mediterranean diet is a predominantly plant-centered eating pattern focused on whole or minimally processed foods. Refined grains, added sugars, and unhealthy fats take a back seat. Portion sizes tend to be smaller, with a focus on enjoying every bite. This aligns with the values of sustainability, community, physical activity, and savoring life's simple pleasures - all integral to the sunny Mediterranean lifestyle.

Since the 1950s, researchers have studied Mediterranean eating patterns and found lower rates of chronic diseases like heart disease, diabetes, and dementia among these populations. The diet is associated with increased longevity, a healthy body weight, and improved quality of life. The abundance of antioxidants, anti-inflammatory fats, fiber, and phytochemicals in fresh plant foods offers protection against many diseases. Swapping out red meat for fish and poultry also confers health perks. Let's review some of the top benefits of following this time-tested diet and lifestyle:

Reduced risk of heart disease.

Replacing saturated fat with monounsaturated fats like olive oil can improve cholesterol levels and lower blood pressure, reducing your risk of heart attack and stroke. Eating more fruits, vegetables, whole grains and omega-3 rich fish provide additional protection.

Lower diabetes risk.

The Mediterranean diet helps regulate blood sugar levels, due to the combination of healthy fats, protein, and fiber-rich complex carbs that stabilize glucose levels. Refined carbs and sugar are limited.

Cancer prevention.

Antioxidants in fruits, vegetables, herbs and olive oil help protect cells from damage that can cause cancer. Less processed meat also reduces risk.

Brain health.

Fish, olive oil, nuts and seeds provide omega-3 fatty acids and vitamin E that may enhance cognitive abilities, memory and learning.

Weight loss.

An abundance of fruits, vegetables and whole foods keeps you feeling full. Moderate calories from healthy fats and smaller portions also facilitate a healthy weight.

Mood boost.

Limiting sugar and emphasizing fruits, vegetables and whole grains improves energy levels. Healthy fats benefit brain function and may reduce depression risk.

Longevity.

Adhering to this diet is associated with lower risk of death from any cause, plus increased lifespan. Lifestyle factors like more physical activity and social connection also promote longevity.

Clearly, the whole-foods focused Mediterranean diet offers head-to-toe benefits for optimal health. While transitioning to this new approach takes some effort, think of it as an investment in yourself. Follow the medically-backed guidance in this book to make lasting improvements to your eating habits, vitality, and joie de vivre. An inspiring journey awaits!

Health Benefits of the Mediterranean Diet

The Mediterranean diet has been associated with a wide range of health benefits, largely attributed to its emphasis on plant-based foods, healthy fats, and lifestyle components like physical activity and community. Adopting this way of eating can have profound protective effects against chronic diseases and support healthy aging.

In study after study, populations following traditional Mediterranean diets have lower rates of heart disease and stroke compared to those eating standard Western diets. One seminal study on the island of Crete in the 1960s revealed very low rates of heart disease, spurring decades of research on the Mediterranean diet's cardiovascular benefits.

The diet provides heart-helping omega-3 fatty acids from fish, monounsaturated fats from olive oil and nuts, and antioxidants from fruits and vegetables. It's naturally lower in artery-clogging saturated fat and rich in fiber. Together, these nutrients reduce systemic inflammation, improve cholesterol levels, decrease blood pressure, and support healthy blood flow.

The Mediterranean style of eating has also been linked with better blood sugar control and a reduced risk of developing type 2 diabetes. Replacing refined grains with whole grains and emphasizing produce provides steady, slow-releasing carbohydrates. Healthy fats like olive oil and omega-3s improve insulin sensitivity. The overall dietary pattern of the Mediterranean diet supports steady energy and balanced blood sugar.

Additionally, studies associate the Mediterranean diet with lower risks for certain cancers, especially colon, prostate, and breast cancers. The plethora of antioxidants, polyphenols, and phytochemicals in plant foods help remove harmful free radicals, reducing cellular damage that can lead to cancer formation. Fiber is also protective against colorectal cancers. The anti-inflammatory effects of the diet further deter cancer growth factors.

The Mediterranean diet may benefit brain health as well. Higher adherence to this eating pattern has been associated with slower rates of cognitive decline and lower dementia risk. The mono- and polyunsaturated fatty acids provide structural brain support and help reduce inflammation. Antioxidants protect delicate brain tissue while vitamins and nutrients nourish neurons. Increased blood flow benefits cognition too. Even neurodegenerative diseases like Parkinson's and Alzheimer's may be delayed by this diet.

Beyond specific conditions, the Mediterranean diet facilitates healthy aging and longevity. The prevalence of nutrient-rich plant foods fights cellular aging due to their antioxidant, anti-inflammatory properties. Vibrant wellbeing into older age allows continued independence and engagement with life. Traditional Mediterranean cultures value elders as honored members of multi-generational families and communities.

Weight loss is another potential perk of the Mediterranean diet. While not overtly restrictive, emphasizing produce, legumes, and fiber creates meals with lower calorie density compared to Western diets of processed foods. Protein from plant and seafood sources improves satiety between meals. Monounsaturated fats like olive oil also increase satiety and facilitate nutrient absorption. An active lifestyle intrinsic to Mediterranean cultures boosts calorie burning too. For lasting success, the diet promotes positive relationships with food instead of deprivation.

The totality of the Mediterranean diet and lifestyle provides multi-pronged benefits for long-term wellbeing. No single "superfood" is responsible - rather, the synergistic combination of minimally processed plant foods, healthy fats, anti-inflammatory properties, satisfying meals, and active lifestyle work together to support optimal health. Pairing this ancient eating wisdom with modern science can help prevent chronic disease while enjoying food.

Adopting the Mediterranean diet requires adapting thinking around food. Instead of a quick fuel stop, value it as a source of nourishment to relish and share. Savor colorful produce, quality fats, whole grains, and mindfully prepared meals. Food is healthiest when enjoyed in moderation with appreciation and connection. Seek balance, variety and freshness. Portions of sweets or red meat can be incorporated at times without detriment if the overall eating pattern remains Mediterranean focused.

Begin gradually transitioning to this style of eating, focusing first on increasing vegetables, fruits, beans, lentils, whole grains and healthy fats like olive oil, avocados and nuts. Gradually reduce refined carbs and sugars, and be mindful of saturated fat from meat and full-fat dairy. With practice, the principles of the Mediterranean diet become second nature. Exploring new produce, flavors and recipes makes healthy eating fun.

While research continues illuminating the Mediterranean diet's health powers, current evidence strongly supports its benefits. Protecting your heart, brain, cells and total wellbeing starts on your plate. Embrace this time-tested diet and lifestyle for lifelong vibrancy.

How to Adopt the Mediterranean Lifestyle

Shifting to a Mediterranean style of eating and living offers tremendous benefits, from weight loss to reduced disease risk, but changing lifelong habits can feel daunting. Many become discouraged thinking this way of life is complicated or unrealistic for their current routine. However, incremental changes focused on adding in more of the good stuff rather than banning foods leads to sustainable success.

First, emphasize abundance of plant foods. Gradually increase your vegetable and fruit quantities until you reach at least five servings of vegetables and two servings of fruit daily. Try showcasing produce by adding mushrooms, peppers, onions and greens to omelets. Blend berries into smoothies or layer banana slices and peanut butter onto whole grain toast. Roast cauliflower or Brussels sprouts to flavorful caramelization or sauté zucchini ribbons in olive oil.

Discover new-to-you produce like artichokes, figs, or starfruit and investigate lesser-known grains like farro, quinoa and amaranth. Herbs and spices like basil, oregano, cumin and cinnamon liven up dishes while slicing veggies ahead makes grab and go snacking simpler. Include beans, lentils or tofu in soups and stews for protein and fiber. Slowly expanding your produce palette makes achieving higher daily quantities effortless.

Next up is exchanging butter and vegetable oils for healthy fats like olive, avocado and nut oils. Extra virgin olive oil becomes your staple for drizzling, sautéing, roasting and dressings. Nutrient rich avocados smash onto whole grain toast or swirl into smoothies. Nuts and seeds sprinkle over salads, blend into pesto or give toast some crunch.

These fats satiate while providing key nutrients and antioxidants. Even just using olive oil when cooking starts conferring advantages. Play with new to you varieties like pistachio, hazelnut or walnut oils to ignite your taste buds.

Increasing seafood intake to twice weekly propagates essential omega-3s. Varying fish like rich salmon, meaty tuna and inexpensive sardines prevents boredom. Quick cooking options like sautéing whitefish with lemon or baking cod over spinach streamline prep. Canned tuna mixed with olive oil and herbs makes an easy protein packed salad topping.

Seeking sustainability certified seafood ensures healthy oceans for the future. If plant-based proteins better suit your lifestyle, incorporate lentils, chickpeas and tofu frequently.

Limiting intake of processed sugars, refined grains and heavy meats encourages weight loss and optimizes health. Satisfy occasional sweet cravings with fresh fruits like oranges, figs or dates. When a bakery treat is in order, share it with a friend or freeze half for later.

Substitute whole grain versions of bread, rice and pasta in favorite recipes. Rely more on beans, vegetables and smaller meat portions in tacos, soups and pastas. Portion control and mindfulness, savoring each bite, prevents overeating.

Social, relaxed eating is integral to the Mediterranean lifestyle. Set the table nicely even for casual meals. Share meals with loved ones when possible, conversing and laughing together. Don't eat on the run - sit down and appreciate every flavorful bite. Sipping herbal tea after dinner extends that warm time together.

Incorporate activity you enjoy like walking, cycling or gardening into daily routines rather than stringent exercise regimens. Find stress reducing strategies that work for you, perhaps yoga, meditation, massage or soothing music.

Aim for eight hours of sleep nightly and take time to enjoy hobbies that bring you joy. View these lifestyle shifts as adding in energizing habits rather than restrictive ones. Each positive change compounds, creating momentum that keeps you moving forward on the path toward better wellbeing.

The Mediterranean lifestyle beautifully nourishes body and spirit. Its flexible framework allows customization around preferences and restrictions so anyone can experience its benefits. Relish this joyful journey of discovery in eating, activity and living with greater intention.

Budget-Friendly Tips for the Mediterranean Diet

Eating well doesn't have to break the bank. With rising food costs and busy schedules, sticking to a budget can seem at odds with making healthy choices. But with a bit of planning, creativity and know-how, you can follow a Mediterranean diet on any budget. This chapter will provide money-saving strategies to help you fill your kitchen with delicious, nutrient-dense foods without overspending. You'll discover how to shop smart, substitute pricier items, batch prep meals, and repurpose leftovers into new dishes.

First, let's review some of the basic principles. As a reminder, the Mediterranean diet emphasizes vegetables, fruits, whole grains, beans, lentils, nuts, seeds, herbs, spices and olive oil. It limits red meat in favor of fish and poultry. Wine is enjoyed in moderation with meals. While fresh, high-quality ingredients are ideal, frozen and canned options ensure you always have nutrient-rich foods on hand. With a well-stocked pantry and freezer, you can whip up fast, affordable meals anytime.

When shopping, be selective - choose seasonal produce at its peak, which is fresher and less expensive. Stick to basic whole grains like brown rice and oats rather than specialty products. Purchase olive oil from discount grocers; buy in bulk when possible. Canned tuna, eggs, plain Greek yogurt and legumes provide lean protein for pennies per serving. Make meat stretch further by using it in small amounts to flavor soups, grains and vegetables rather than as the main component.

Get the most nutrition for your money by focusing on fruits and veggies in a range of colors - deep greens, reds, oranges, purples. Each provides a unique set of antioxidants and phytonutrients to protect your health. When pricier berries aren't in the budget, banana and apples make nutritious substitutes. Canned and frozen options are just as healthy. Beans, lentils and tofu offer inexpensive vegetarian protein.

Batch cooking saves time and money. Make extra grains, roasted veggies or soup on the weekend to enjoy throughout the week. Soups, stews and casseroles often taste better as leftovers. Portion out and freeze individual servings for quick heat-and-eat meals later. Repurpose leftovers in creative new dishes - for example, roast chicken one night, shred and add to a salad or soup the next.

Planning ahead and shopping with a list prevents impulse purchases and food waste. Check circulars and only buy what you need for the week. Incorporate more meatless meals based around beans, eggs, whole grains and veggies to save money. Enjoy fruit for dessert rather than pricey sweets. Snack on small amounts of nuts and homemade popcorn versus packaged treats. Bring lunch to work to save on eating out. With a few simple habits, you'll find this diet very budget-friendly.

The Mediterranean diet offers an optimal approach for health and longevity. While enhancing your pantry with nutrient-rich foods requires an initial investment, the long-term dividends for your wellbeing are priceless. Approaching this lifestyle gradually allows you to identify the changes with the biggest impact for your health and budget. As the principles become second nature, you'll discover how to eat deliciously on a budget. Savvy shopping, batch cooking and creative repurposing of leftovers into new meals will become habit. You'll look and feel better without breaking the bank. A nutritious Mediterranean diet is within reach for any budget!

Time Management and Meal Planning Strategies

Finding time to prepare healthy Mediterranean meals can be a challenge with a busy schedule. However, with some planning and efficiency in the kitchen, it is possible to reap the benefits of this diet even during your busiest days. A little strategy goes a long way when it comes to meal prepping Mediterranean style.

Start by taking stock of your weekly commitments and identifying any pockets of time you can dedicate to food preparation. This may be Sunday afternoons or a couple of hours one weekday evening. Try to find at least 2-3 hours to do recipe planning, grocery shopping and some cooking.

When you have time to prep, make big batches of Mediterranean diet staples like roasted vegetables, cooked grains, beans, lentils, and dressings. Portion these out to pull together quick meals later in the week. Having prepped ingredients ready to go is key for assembling healthy Mediterranean dishes with minimal effort.

Get your kitchen set up for efficiency. Store main equipment like pots, pans, knives, cutting boards and utensils within easy reach. Have herbs, spices, oils and commonly used ingredients organized for fast access. Sharpen knives ahead of time. Clear clutter and streamline work zones. With a functional cooking space, you can work more quickly and fluidly.

When shopping, stick to the perimeter of the store where whole foods like produce, proteins, dairy are located. Limit time in aisles to just grab some grains, oils, spices and other Mediterranean diet essentials. Make a list grouped by store section to minimize backtracking.

Embrace one-pot meals, casseroles, sheet pan dinners and slow cooker dishes that require little hands-on time after prepping ingredients.pressure cooker and Instant Pot recipes prepare beans, grains, and soups in a fraction of traditional cook times.

Cook once, eat twice by doubling recipes when possible to use leftovers later in the week. Transform leftovers into new meals—for example, roast chicken one night can become chicken salad or soup later on.

Take advantage of time-saving appliances like food processors, immersion blenders, rice cookers, and electric pressure cookers. Let the tools do some of the work!

Cook quick-cooking proteins like shrimp, white fish, eggs or prepared chicken sausages to pair with veggies, greens and whole grains. Keep frozen precooked proteins like chicken strips on hand for fast meals too.

Prep washed greens and precut vegetables on less busy days to throw together salads and sides effortlessly. Cleaned, dried greens stay fresh for up to 5 days. Precut carrots, peppers, broccoli, cauliflower, etc. make cooking so much faster.

Stock your freezer with peeled/precut bananas, chopped herbs, extra soup portions, meatballs, and other Mediterranean diet recipes. Thaw for instant healthy meals.

Make large batches of homemade dressings, dips, sauces, and spread to enjoy throughout the week. These flavor boosters make it easy to liven up simple dishes.

Enjoy Mediterranean diet-approved convenience foods in moderation—canned beans, precooked quinoa, jarred marinated vegetables, frozen fruits and veggies—to supplement homemade dishes.

Meal prep a few dishes on less busy days to reheat and eat later in the week. Prepared meals can be grab-and-go for busy mornings.

Let family members help! Having everyone chop vegetables or shred chicken can turn meal prep into quality time.

Above all, focus on eating the Mediterranean way rather than perfectly replicating traditional cuisine every day. Satisfying meals can be simple, like greens with canned beans and store-bought rotisserie chicken. The health benefits stem from the overall eating pattern.

With a few tricks, planning, and efficient prep, you can enjoy wholesome Mediterranean meals even during your busiest times. The investment of time pays off with meals that nurture lasting wellness.

CHAPTER 1

THE FUNDAMENTALS OF THE MEDITERRANEAN DIET

Essential Ingredients in the Mediterranean Diet

The Mediterranean diet derives immense flavor from simple, high quality ingredients. As you stock your kitchen, focus first on staples that form the foundation of this eating pattern. Building meals and snacks from these wholesome foods makes adopting Mediterranean style effortless.

Extra virgin olive oil provides the cornerstone. It tops salads, marinates proteins, sautés veggies and more while delivering healthy fats. When purchasing, select a bottled oil packaged in dark glass and labeled extra virgin. This indicates first cold pressing and optimum flavor. Seek a harvest date within the past year for freshness. Spend a bit more on quality if possible as cheap oils may be diluted with other lesser ones.

A complex peppery flavor with aromas of grass or fruit signals nuanced taste perfect for drizzling over finished dishes. More mild, buttery oils suit cooking. Olive oil solidifies in cold temperatures but rebounds once warmed. Store in a cool cupboard away from light to maximize longevity.

Canned or jarred tomatoes are indispensable Mediterranean ingredients. They lend rich sweetness to soups, stews, pastas, pizzas and more. Canned whole tomatoes should be pulpy and tender. Chopped or crushed canned tomatoes provide convenience. Select low sodium or no salt added products and brands packed in juice rather than puree for fullest tomato essence.

When tomatoes are in season, freeze batches of fresh sauce and diced tomatoes to harness that summery vibrance year round. Herbs like basil, oregano and thyme permit deeply savory dishes. Grow them fresh or purchase dried.

Lemons bring brightness to both sweet and savory recipes. Their juice provides tangy balance while zest imparts citrus flair. Store fruits loosely bagged in the crisper drawer up to two weeks. Bottled juice maintains freshness for months in the fridge. Lemon juice concentrates flavor in marinades, dressings and sauces.

Garlic, onions and shallots form the aromatic base of countless Mediterranean recipes. Their pungent punch enhances everything from soups to dips. Store whole bulbs and onions in a cool, dry spot with good ventilation. Refrigerate pre-peeled cloves.

Yogurt contains beneficial probiotics that support gut and immune health. Seek plain nonfat Greek varieties packing protein too. Sheep or goat milk yogurts offer a tasty twist. Whisk in herbs, lemon and garlic for a quick veggie dip or fruit topping. Blend yogurt into smoothies for a protein boost.

Hearty whole grains like bulgur, farro, barley and brown rice make satisfying side dishes or salad toppers. Their fiber content keeps you fuller longer while providing sustained energy. Cook a big batch of whole grains on weekends for quick lunches throughout the week.

Nuts and seeds lend crunch, flavor and nutrition. Almonds, walnuts, pistachios, pine nuts and pumpkin seeds show up frequently in Mediterranean cuisine. Store them in airtight containers to prevent rancidity. Enjoy a small handful for a nutritious snack anytime.

Pulses like lentils, chickpeas, white beans and peas provide ample plant-based protein and fiber. Canned options offer fast convenience, but cooking dried beans from scratch is inexpensive while allowing control over sodium content. Simmer beans from scratch in big batches and freeze portioned quantities for later. Add pulses to soups, stews, pastas, rice bowls, salads and more.

Fresh fruits and vegetables in season highlight nature's bounty. Leafy greens, brussels sprouts, broccoli, green beans, peppers, mushrooms, summer squash, berries and more grace Mediterranean meals. Weekly trips to farmer's markets help you take advantage of peak ripeness. Freeze or preserve surplus crops during growing months.

Seafood, especially fatty fish like salmon, tuna, mackerel and sardines, delivers anti-inflammatory omega-3 fatty acids. Seek out sustainable options when possible. Canned fish like tuna and sardines make cost-effective options to keep on hand.

Poultry, eggs and cheese offer lean protein. Chicken, turkey and duck can be sautéed, roasted or grilled. Eggs conveniently prepare anytime. Parmesan, feta and goat cheeses crumble nicely over dishes.

You don't have to hunt down speciality products to eat Mediterranean. Focus on including these staples into your weekly shopping routine and you'll always be equipped to create delicious, fresh meals.

Stock your cupboards, fridge and freezer with olive oil, whole grains, nuts, canned fish, herbs and spices.

Keep lemons, garlic, plain yogurt, eggs, cheese and fresh seasonal produce on hand.

Shop for any favorites you may miss like whole wheat pasta, brown rice, or beans.

Supplement with items like canned tomatoes, foreign cheeses or trendy grains like farro as desired over time.

Planning meals around vibrant, minimally processed Mediterranean staples naturally guides you toward abundant nutrition and scrumptious home cooking. With a well stocked kitchen, you're on your way to effortlessly infusing this healthful way of eating into everyday life.

Reading and Understanding Food Labels

When transitioning to a Mediterranean diet, reading nutrition labels is an indispensable skill. With so many claims plastered across food packaging, it can be confusing to know which products actually align with a whole foods diet. This chapter will help you become an expert label reader, able to decode marketing hype and identify truly healthy options. You'll learn how to spot hidden sugars, unhealthy fats, and unnecessary additives to make optimal choices.

First, let's review the Mediterranean diet principles. This eating pattern emphasizes whole, unprocessed foods like fruits, vegetables, legumes, whole grains, nuts, seeds, herbs, and olive oil. It limits sugar, refined grains, unhealthy fats, and highly processed foods. With this framework in mind, we can approach a nutrition label with a discerning eye.

Start by looking at the ingredient list. Ingredients are listed by quantity - the first few should be whole foods like whole grains, beans, nuts, or fruit. Watch for added sugars like cane sugar, corn syrup or honey within the first few ingredients. Artificial colors, preservatives and emulsifiers signal a highly processed food. If you can't recognize or pronounce an ingredient, it's best to avoid it.

Compare the calories and nutrients between different brands and versions of similar products. When comparing yogurts, for instance, choose the option with the highest protein, lowest sugar, and minimal additives. The same applies when comparing breads, cereals, or plant-based milks.

Pay special attention to the serving size listed, as the calories and nutrients are based on one serving. Be aware that packages sometimes contain multiple servings, so you may need to multiply. Limit foods high in saturated fat, added sugars, and sodium. Prioritize options providing fiber, protein, vitamins, and minerals instead.

When evaluating whole grain products, make sure the word "whole" appears before grain ingredients like whole wheat, whole oats, or whole grain corn. Look for at least 3 grams of fiber per serving; this indicates more intact whole grains. For bread, cereals and crackers, aim for less than 150 calories and 5 grams or less added sugar per serving.

Protein sources like yogurt, chicken, and plant-based meat alternatives should have at least 5-10 grams protein per serving. Yogurts should contain live active cultures and minimal added sugars - aim for under 15 grams total carbs. Cheese should be made from milk and salt rather than "cheese product".

Stick to plain nuts and seeds rather than honey roasted or sugary flavors. Dried fruits with no added sweeteners make a better choice than "yogurt-covered" or chocolate-dipped versions. Frozen fruits and veggies with just the fruit or vegetable listed are ideal.

The Mediterranean diet is centered on whole, minimally processed foods. By diligently reading labels rather than marketing claims, you can see through food industry tricks and make informed choices. Base purchases on the quality of ingredients, fiber content, amounts of protein, sugar, and sodium rather than flashy packaging. With practice, you'll become adept at separating health foods from imposters!

Portion Sizes and Meal Timing

The Mediterranean diet is less about strict rules and calorie counting and more about overall eating patterns. However, paying attention to portion sizes and meal frequency can help manage hunger, prevent overeating and aid weight loss efforts. Approach this flexible, intuitive eating style using simple guiding principles.

In the Mediterranean lifestyle, food is meant to be savored rather than rushed. Meals are a pleasant social experience shared with family and friends. Slower eating allows time for your brain to register fullness signals from your stomach. This mindful approach prevents overconsumption.

When plating dishes, visualize filling half your plate with vegetables and fruits. These water- and fiber-rich plant foods aid satiety. Fill a quarter plate with whole grains like brown rice or quinoa. The remaining quarter comprises protein such as beans, lentils, fish or poultry. This balanced plate leads to satisfying, nutrient-dense meals.

Limit red meat to a few times per month, treating it more as a condiment rather than main dish. Portion fish, poultry and eggs modestly, using 3-4 ounces cooked portions. Higher protein needs can be met by increasing plant proteins like beans, nuts and seeds.

Consider volume when portioning meals. Dishes incorporating broth-laden soups, leafy salads, roasted veggies or whole grains feel more plentiful compared to dense options like cheese, meat or creamy pasta. Fill your plate with volume using plant foods.

Dress vegetables and greens with olive oil and acid from lemons or vinegar rather than drenching with dense, heavy sauces. This allows enjoying larger portions of the good stuff!

Reduce portion distortion by using smaller plates and bowls. This prevents heaping excess food that gets mindlessly consumed. Serve dishes family-style instead of pre-plating large portions.

Slow down while eating and savor each bite. Pause between bites, put utensils down, and thoroughly chew food. Take time to appreciate flavors and textures. This mindset prevents overeating.

Drink water with meals and sip slowly rather than gulping. Starting meals with broth-based soup aids satiety too. Herbal tea makes a nice digestive after heavier meals.

Balance meals with healthy snacks to prevent overindulging at main meals. Pair carbohydrates with protein, fiber or healthy fat for satiating snacks like whole grain toast with avocado, oatmeal with nuts and fruit, or yogurt with berries.

Follow the European tradition of multi-course meals if desired. For example, start with a salad, follow with a vegetable side dish and whole grain, then finish with a modest protein. This extends enjoyment.

Typical Mediterranean meal frequency includes a light breakfast, larger lunch, lighter late afternoon snack, and main evening meal. However, modify this to best suit your needs and schedule.

Avoid restrictive dieting. Occasional indulgences in celebration, for holidays, or culturally relevant foods are encouraged within reason. It's an eating pattern for life!

Portion distortion from growing serving sizes makes it hard to recognize true serving sizes today. Use visual cues like a deck of cards for meats or tennis ball for snacks. Follow suggested serving sizes on packages.

Get acquainted with recommended servings of whole grains (1/2 cup cooked), nuts(1 ounce), nut butters (2 tablespoons) and seeds (2-3 tablespoons). Stick to a 1 1/2–2 cup serving of dairy and 2–3 ounces of cheese per day.

Let hunger signals and fullness cues guide portions instead of eating from external cues like finishing everything on your plate. Only take seconds after a reasonable break.

Avoid mindless overconsumption when eating in front of the TV, computer or other distractions. Focus just on the food to become more attuned to satiety signals.

Manage large restaurant portions by boxing up half before eating or splitting dishes with dining partners. Request sauces and dressings on the side.

The Mediterranean lifestyle is driven more by quality than quantity of food. Honor hunger, practice mindfulness, and find joy in meals to naturally regulate portions.

How to Organize Your Kitchen for Success

An organized, well-stocked kitchen makes preparing nutritious Mediterranean meals much more manageable. By setting up your space and staples strategically, you'll remove any friction from eating healthy. These kitchen organization tips will become the foundation empowering your meal planning success.

First, clear clutter from counters and drawers. Donate or trash any old kitchenware you don't use. Designate a spot for everything - pots and pans together, utensils in a crock or drawer, knives on a magnet strip or block. Group like items to optimize efficiency.

Install shelving for spices, oils and other staples to free up cabinet space. Consider open shelving or glass door cabinets to view items easily. Pull seldom used appliances off counters into cabinets, keeping only basics like a kettle, knife block and olive oil cruet visible.

Next, purge and consolidate your pantry. Toss expired items and group like foods together - pastas and grains, oils and vinegars, snacks, canned goods. Use clear bins or jars to locate items at a glance. Keeping your pantry organized prevents buying duplicates and forgetting what's on hand.

Clear out the freezer and fridge too. Toss anything past its prime and wipe down shelves. Group similar items together and keep an inventory list posted on the freezer door to track contents. Place Mediterranean staples like nuts, olives and yogurt toward the front where you'll see them.

Meal plan your week ahead based on grocery store sales or seasonal produce. Post the menu on the fridge or a bulletin board. Make a master grocery list you can tape to the fridge and add to all week. Planning ahead helps you buy only what you need.

To save prep time, prep ingredients in batches on less busy nights to use later in the week. Chop vegetables for easy snacking. Cook a big pot of whole grains to use in multiple meals. Grill extra chicken or steak to top salads.

Stock up on versatile Mediterranean staples when they are on sale. Canned beans, tuna, whole grains and frozen vegetables provide healthy fast options. Dried herbs and spices add flavor to basic dishes.

Keep freshly washed and chopped produce front and center in see-through containers. You'll be much more likely to grab them for snacks and meals when they are visible and ready to eat.

Designate part of a shelf or the door to quick grab breakfast items like yogurt cups, hard boiled eggs and whole grain toast. Build assembling a healthy morning meal into your routine.

Store snacks like nuts, cut up veggies, hummus and fruit at eye level for easy grabbing on the go. Rely on satisfying whole foods rather than processed snack foods when hunger strikes.

Cleaning as you go maintains order. Wash utensils and prep dishes promptly after using them. Set a timer for five minutes before ending cooking to do a quick tidy of the kitchen.

These habits allow you to effortlessly see, access and use Mediterranean ingredients and tools. An organized kitchen minimizes stress and removes obstacles to preparing nourishing meals. Soon your optimized systems will make healthy eating second nature.

Here are some key strategies for Mediterranean diet kitchen organization success:

- Group like items such as oils, spices, canned goods to maximize efficiency.

- Store staples in clear jars or bins so contents are visible at a glance.

- Keep surfaces and drawers clutter free for easier cleaning and cooking.

- Meal plan ahead and shop sales to avoid food waste.

- Prep ingredients in batches to pull together meals quickly.

- Position produce, proteins, snacks prominently for easy grabbing.

- Maintain organization by cleaning up regularly as you cook.

With some thoughtful organization, your kitchen transforms into a smooth running engine powering Mediterranean meal preparation. A streamlined space makes nourishing your body with this incredible diet a sheer joy rather than a chore.

Healthy Snacking on the Mediterranean Diet

Snacking is a great way to refuel between meals and get an energy boost when you need it. But with so many processed snack foods dominating grocery shelves, it can be tricky to find options that align with the Mediterranean diet's focus on whole, nourishing ingredients. This chapter will explore Mediterranean-friendly snacking strategies to keep you satisfied. You'll discover nutritious and convenient snacks to have on hand, and learn how to prepare homemade snacks in advance.

First, let's review the principles of the Mediterranean diet. This lifestyle emphasizes whole foods like vegetables, fruits, legumes, nuts, seeds, whole grains, herbs, spices and olive oil. It limits sugar, refined grains, unhealthy fats and highly processed foods. To make optimal snacking choices, prioritize whole food options with fiber, protein and healthy fats to provide lasting energy.

Fruits and vegetables are always a wise choice. Fresh, in-season produce provides the most nutrients, but frozen, canned and dried options work too. Pair veggies with hummus, guacamole or Greek yogurt dip for a nutrition boost. Apples, bananas, oranges and other fruits make portable snacks. Dried fruits like apricots and dates offer concentrated sweetness, but watch portion sizes as the calories add up quickly.

Nuts and seeds offer protein, healthy fats and vitamins. Measure 1-ounce portions for a satisfying, portable snack. Try different varieties like almonds, pistachios, walnuts, sunflower seeds and pumpkin seeds. Boost the flavor and nutrition by toasting them. You can make your own trail mixes too. Pair with a little dried fruit for natural sweetness.

Popcorn makes a whole grain, fiber-filled snack when air-popped or prepared on the stove with a small amount of olive oil. Sprinkle with nutritional yeast and spices rather than butter for extra flavor. If buying pre-popped, check labels and choose low-sodium, low-fat versions.

Greek yogurt provides filling protein, calcium, probiotics and less sugar than regular yogurt. Opt for plain, unsweetened varieties and add your own fresh fruit, nuts and seeds. Cottage cheese is another high protein snack.

For an energy-boosting snack, blend up homemade smoothies with fruits, veggies, Greek yogurt, nut butter or chia seeds. You control the ingredients, so they align perfectly with a Mediterranean diet.

When prepping snacks in advance, hard boil a dozen eggs and keep them in the fridge to grab and go. Roast a batch of chickpeas with olive oil and spices for a crispy snack throughout the week. Make energy bites by mixing oats, nut butter, Greek yogurt and dried fruit. Portion nuts and seeds into reusable containers for grab-and-go convenience.

Follow these tips to ensure your snacks keep you full and focused between meals, without derailing your healthy Mediterranean diet goals. With a little planning, you'll always have delicious, wholesome snacks on hand to get you through busy days feeling your best.

Thelma Ansen

CHAPTER 2

BREAKFAST RECIPES

Quick and Easy Mediterranean Breakfast Ideas

Starting your day the Mediterranean way sets you up for success. Breakfast fuels energy, satiates hunger, and provides key nutrients to power your morning. Luckily, the Mediterranean diet offers endless options for healthy, satisfying morning meals that can be made quickly even on busy weekdays.

Focus breakfast on fiber, protein and healthy fats to stabilize blood sugar and curb cravings later on. Incorporate vegetables and fruit for essential antioxidants and phytochemicals too.

For effortless mornings, prepare make-ahead dishes to enjoy throughout the week. Boil eggs, cook a big batch of oatmeal, roast sweet potatoes, or blend up chia pudding. Pair these with nuts, seeds, fresh fruit or a dollop of yogurt for well-rounded breakfasts.

Whole grain toast topped with mashed avocado, sautéed mushrooms, smashed beans, or hummus makes another fast Mediterranean breakfast. Add sprouts, tomatoes or a fried egg for extra nutrition.

Wake up to a fruit and yogurt parfait layered with roasted nuts and seeds for protein. Swap in chia or flaxseed pudding if yogurt doesn't agree with you.

Lean into vegetables for morning nutrition. Enjoy leftover roasted veggies atop a bed of greens with olive oil, lemon, salt and pepper. Roast tomatoes, mushrooms, onions, peppers or eggplant ahead of time.

Spread some hummus on a whole wheat wrap. Load up with sliced cucumbers, tomatoes, peppers and sprouts.

Make a savory Mediterranean breakfast hash with potatoes or sweet potatoes, peppers, spinach, onions, beans, eggs and herbs. Serve with avocado, hot sauce and lime.

Cook a batch of steel cut oats or amaranth on your day off for grab-and-go breakfasts throughout the week. Top with bananas, berries, shredded coconut, nuts, seeds or cinnamon.

Pair Greek yogurt or cottage cheese with fresh fruit, nuts and ground flax or chia seeds for a protein and fiber-rich morning meal.

Whisk eggs with diced tomatoes, spinach, feta and herbs, then bake in muffin tins for easy Mediterranean egg muffins. Enjoy with fruit.

Blend banana, berries, greens, nut butter and chia seeds into a creamy, fruity smoothie. Rotate other fruits and veggies too.

Make a veggie frittata with tomatoes, spinach, artichokes and feta or goat cheese. Cut into wedges for quick reheating during the week.

Bake a batch of whole grain muffins using almond flour, oats and fruit. Enjoy with nuts and Greek yogurt for a balanced breakfast.

Top thick sliced multigrain bread with smashed white beans, sautéed kale and a sprinkling of parmesan for a savory toast.

Fold eggs, sautéed peppers, onions, mushrooms and greens into a whole wheat wrap with crumbled feta for a hearty breakfast burrito.

Cook quinoa flakes or amaranth porridge in nondairy milk. Top with chopped nuts, seeds, coconut and fruit for added nutrition and texture.

Make a breakfast bowl with brown rice, roasted squash, greens, chickpeas and tahini. Top with a fried or poached egg.

Heat up leftover soup or stew for a warm, comforting morning meal full of veggies. Pair with avocado toast or breakfast potatoes.

Don't overlook canned fish for easy protein. Top whole grain toast with sardines, smoked trout or salmon.

Keep pre-portioned frozen berry smoothie packs in the freezer. Add milk, yogurt or juice and blend for fast vitamin-rich drinks.

Stir chickpea flour into eggs to make veggie-packed Mediterranean chickpea omelets. Serve with olives, feta and fresh tomatoes.

With the right strategies, preparing Mediterranean breakfasts during busy mornings is totally doable. Embrace leftovers, prepped foods and grab-and-go items for effortless mornings.

Delicious and Nutritious Smoothies

Blending up a delicious smoothie makes enjoying an abundance of fruits and vegetables effortless. These chilled drinks provide ideal on-the-go Mediterranean diet nutrition for busy mornings or snack time. Endless flavor combinations suit any palette while packing in produce for a healthy boost.

Fruits build the base for wholesome smoothies. Berries like strawberries, blueberries, blackberries and raspberries provide sweetness along with antioxidants. Bananas add creaminess and potassium. Citrus fruits like oranges or mangoes incorporate refreshing brightness.

Use frozen fruits to achieve a thicker, chillier texture without diluting flavor. They also allow enjoying out of season produce year round. Let frozen fruits partially thaw 10 minutes before blending for easier mixing.

Vegetables blend easily into smoothies without overpowering sweet fruit flavors. Spinach, kale and swiss chard pack a big nutritional punch while their bold flavors fade into the background. Carrots add vitamin A and natural sweetness. Avocado lends a rich, creamy mouthfeel.

For the health conscious, teaspoons of fresh ginger or turmeric add anti-inflammatory benefits. Green powders like spirulina and wheatgrass provide concentrated vitamins and minerals.

Nuts, seeds and nut butters integrate protein, fiber and healthy fats to keep you satisfied. Almond butter pairs perfectly with berries. Chia or hemp seeds thicken smoothies' texture. Toasting nuts intensifies their flavor before blending.

Dairy and non-dairy milks thin out thick smoothies. Opt for unsweetened varieties of almond, soy, coconut, oat or dairy milk. Plain kefir or Greek yogurt contribute protein and tang.

Cool smoothies quickly by using frozen fruits and milk. Adding a handful of ice if needed avoids diluting flavors. Bananas, avocados and nut butters provide natural creaminess.

For deeper flavor, begin with strongly brewed coffee, tea, cocoa or herbal teas like rooibos or hibiscus. Spices like cinnamon, nutmeg, ginger and cardamom add interest. Vanilla or almond extract infuses a lovely aroma.

Make smoothiesHearty enough for a meal by including protein, fiber and healthy fats. Mix in nut butters, avocado, thick yogurts, chia seeds or wheat germ. Heartier smoothies sustain energy longer.

Dress up your smoothie glass with fun toppings. Sprinkle chia seeds, shredded coconut, cocoa nibs or crushed nuts on top for crunch. Drizzle nut butters, honey or agave for extra sweetness.

Prep smoothie ingredients in weekly batches for grab and go convenience. Wash and chop produce before freezing in portions. Measure nut butters, chia seeds and milks into individual containers to simply dump and blend.

Here are some delicious Mediterranean diet smoothie ingredient combinations:

- Strawberry, banana, almond butter, almond milk

- Blueberry, kale, vanilla Greek yogurt, honey

- Mango, pineapple, coconut water, chia seeds

- Peach, raspberry, spinach, vanilla whey protein, ice

- Pomegranate, carrot, orange juice, ginger

- Acai powder, cocoa powder, avocado, coconut milk

With endless tasty combinations, smoothies make it tempting to load up on fruits, veggies and nutrition each day. Blend your way to a vibrant Mediterranean diet.

Whole Grain and Seed-Packed Recipes

Whole grains and seeds are nutritional powerhouses that play a starring role in the Mediterranean diet. Teeming with fiber, protein, healthy fats and key micronutrients, they provide sustained energy while protecting your health. This chapter will explore ways to incorporate more whole grains and seeds into your daily meals and snacks. You'll discover new ingredients to try, tips for preparing them, and delicious recipes to add to your repertoire.

First, let's review the basics. Whole grains like oats, brown rice, quinoa, bulgur and farro retain all their natural bran and germ, making them more nutritious than refined grains. They take a bit longer to cook but are worth the wait. Seeds like chia, flax, hemp, pumpkin and sunflower provide plant-based protein and omega-3 fatty acids. Combining whole grains and seeds ensures your meals stay power-packed.

Try substituting whole grain pasta, brown rice, quinoa or bulgur in favorite recipes, or use half whole grain and half white to transition your palate. Hearty whole grains make satisfying breakfast porridges or can be used in pilafs, risottos or mixed into salads. Seeds lend texture and crunch when sprinkled on yogurt, oatmeal or salads.

Soak dry beans, lentils and whole grains like quinoa overnight to reduce cooking times. Make extra grains and beans to use throughout the week in meals and snacks. Get creative with leftovers - for example, toss cooked grains or pulses with roasted veggies, marinara sauce and cheese for a quick grain bowl.

Take advantage of your slow cooker or pressure cooker to effortlessly prepare hearty bean and whole grain dishes while you're out.steel-cut oats

Try new ancient grains like amaranth, sorghum, spelt and teff for nutrients and texture. Pair with nuts, seeds, beans or sautéed veggies for delicious, hearty meals.

Don't limit whole grains to savory dishes - use them in muffins, pancakes, energy bars and breads too. Substitute up to half the all-purpose flour in recipes with whole wheat or oat flour. Add sunflower or pumpkin seeds for a nourishing crunch.

Here are some Mediterranean diet-approved recipes to try:

- Overnight oats with chia seeds, nuts and fresh fruit

- Hearty vegetable and bean soup over farro

- Quinoa tabbouleh salad with parsley, tomatoes, cucumbers

- Curried lentils and brown rice with garam masala

- Savory steel-cut oatmeal topped with spinach, mushrooms, and a fried egg

- Zucchini muffins made with whole wheat flour and walnuts

Incorporating more whole grains and seeds provides a big nutritional payoff. Let these nourishing ingredients play a starring role in your Mediterranean diet for vibrant health!

Egg-Based Mediterranean Dishes

Eggs are a versatile and nutritious Mediterranean diet staple. As a complete protein containing all nine essential amino acids, eggs support energy, muscle health and satiety. They also provide vitamin D, selenium, lutein and zeaxanthin antioxidants. Enjoyed in moderation, eggs make a great addition to the Mediterranean diet. Here are some delicious ways to incorporate them for breakfast, lunch or dinner:

Frittatas – Bake eggs mixed with Mediterranean veggies like spinach, tomatoes, artichokes, onions or peppers. Add feta, goat or parmesan cheese. Serve wedges for meals throughout the week.

Veggie omelets – Lightly beat eggs then sauté with fresh veggies like mushrooms, peppers, greens and herbs. Top with avocado or hummus and feta.

Egg muffins - Grease a muffin tin then crack an egg into each well. Add diced veggies, cheese, meat or beans. Bake until set and enjoy on-the-go.

Breakfast bowls – Cooked grains like quinoa or farro topped with sautéed veggies, greens, beans and a poached or fried egg. Finish with herbs, hot sauce or tahini.

Shakshuka – Poach eggs in a skillet of simmering tomato sauce seasoned with cumin, paprika and cayenne. Serve with crusty bread.

Greek eggs - Sauté onions and greens in olive oil. Add eggs and cook until set, then finish with diced tomatoes, olives, feta and fresh herbs.

Huevos rancheros - Layer cooked black beans, salsa, fried eggs and avocado over corn tortillas for a Mediterranean twist on this classic.

Asparagus and egg breakfast tacos - Sauté asparagus and onions, fold in eggs, and wrap in whole grain tortillas with feta crumbles.

Baked egg cups - Line muffin tin with eggplant slices, crack an egg into each cup, and bake until set. Remove cups and dress with tzatziki.

Mediterranean omelet or sandwich filling - Sauté eggplant, peppers, onions and spinach. Add eggs and cook, then stuff into a pita or whole grain sandwich bread.

Savory breakfast casserole - Combine eggs, cottage cheese, roasted veggies and herbs. Pour into a baking dish, top with cheese and bake until set.

Sweet potato hash with eggs - Sauté cubed sweet potatoes, peppers, spinach and onions. Make wells to crack eggs into and cook until desired doneness.

Fried eggs over hummus toast - Spread whole grain toast with hummus, then fry an egg to place on top. Finish with spices like sumac, za'atar or red pepper flakes.

Egg drop soup - Whisk eggs with stock, herbs and lemon, then gradually pour into simmering broth while stirring to form egg ribbons.

Herbed Mediterranean eggs - Poach or fry eggs, then top with a mixture of chopped tomatoes, cucumbers, olives, herbs and drizzled olive oil.

Spanish tortilla - Sauté potatoes and onions, combine with beaten eggs and bake into a frittata/quiche hybrid. Cut into wedges.

Beet pickled eggs - Hard boil and pickle eggs in a mixture of beet juice, vinegar, garlic, bay leaves and black peppercorns for a beautiful hue.

Herbed avocado toast with eggs - Mash avocado with lemon juice, garlic and herbs, then top whole grain or seed bread with egg cooked to your liking.

With minimal time and effort, eggs can be transformed into Mediterranean masterpieces perfectly suited for any meal or occasion.

Meal Prep Tips for Busy Mornings

Mornings often feel rushed, making it tempting to grab an unhealthy convenient breakfast. However, a little strategic preparation allows you to fuel busy days with nourishing Mediterranean meals, even when time is tight. Follow these tips to assemble quick, satisfying breakfasts.

Prep ingredients ahead on less hectic evenings to build meals efficiently in the morning. Cook a big batch of whole grains like quinoa, brown rice or oatmeal on your next day off. Portion into individual containers ready to reheat. You can also pre-chop veggies for easy egg scrambles or bake a batch of whole grain breakfast bars.

Wash and chop fruits and vegetables when you return from the grocery store. Store prepped ingredients in containers in the fridge to simply grab. Precut melons, fresh berries, bell peppers and mushrooms save minutes in the morning.

Make a week's worth of overnight oats in mason jars on Sunday. Combine oats, chia seeds, milk and fruits like berries in jars. Refrigerate overnight so you have grab-and-go parfaits ready to enjoy without any morning prep.

Hard boil a dozen eggs on the weekend for quick protein all week long. Enjoy plain, slice over salads or add to whole grain toast. You can also prep egg muffin cups with your favorite veggies and cheese that reheat easily.

Wake up 10 minutes earlier and use the time to get breakfast components ready while the coffee brews. Set the table, reheat oatmeal and slice fruit so it's ready to eat when you sit down. Those 10 minutes prevent rushing.

Invest in a good blender, waffle iron or griddle so you can whip up smoothies, whole grain waffles or veggie frittatas quickly. Having the right kitchen tools on hand facilitates fast cooking.

Shop specifically for easy breakfast items like yogurt cups, whole grain cereal or bread, frozen veggie mixes and fresh fruit. Stocking the right Mediterranean foods avoids grabbing pastries on the go.

Prep lunch ingredients the night before too so your morning involves grabbing breakfast and lunch to go. Build a healthy habit of packing meals rather than buying them.

Wake up early risers first to start breakfast while you get ready. Older kids can reheat oatmeal and slice fruit with minimal supervision.

Set up a breakfast station or cart with supplies ready to assemble meals efficiently. Stock it with dishes, utensils, spices, oils, fruit, bread for quick grabbing.

Planning is essential for healthy Mediterranean breakfasts on busy mornings. But with the right strategies in place, you can build the habit of nourishing, sit-down meals to start each day right even on the busiest mornings.

CHAPTER 3

LUNCH RECIPES

Simple Salads and Dressings

Fresh, vibrant salads make frequent appearances in the Mediterranean diet. Heaping platters of greens, vegetables, beans, and perhaps some olives, cheese or tuna are often served as a first course or light lunch. Salads provide a perfect opportunity to highlight the bounty of seasonal produce. The key is keeping both salads and dressings simple, allowing the quality ingredients to shine. This chapter will explore easy salad building blocks and techniques for creating balanced Mediterranean-style salads.

Let's start with the base. Mixed greens like romaine, arugula, spinach and kale supply nutrient-dense leaves. Romaine's crunchy texture makes a nice foundation. Baby spinach offers tender leaves that wilt slightly under heated ingredients. Bitter greens like arugula and frisée provide counterpoints to sweet vegetables and fruits.

Beyond lettuces, explore other greens like shredded cabbage, kale, chard, or peppery watercress. You can also use whole-grain bases like cooked farro, wheat berries, or quinoa for hearty main dish salads.

When adding vegetables, think variety. Chopped cucumbers, tomatoes, carrots, bell peppers, and radishes add color, flavor, and textures. Roasted vegetables like zucchini, eggplant, mushrooms and asparagus contribute warm, caramelized notes. Beans, chickpeas or lentils add protein and substance. Fresh herbs like parsley, basil, dill or mint brighten up greens.

For Mediterranean flair, include ingredients like artichoke hearts, olives, capers, and roasted red peppers. Crumbled feta, Parmesan or goat cheese offer briny, creamy accents. Nuts and seeds add crunch. If desired, top salads with grilled chicken or seafood.

The dressing possibilities are endless. A classic vinaigrette pairs fruity olive oil with an acid like vinegar or lemon juice. Add zesty herbs and spices like garlic, mustard, basil or oregano. Blend in yogurt or tahini for a luscious, creamy dressing. For richness, whisk in some crumbled feta or goat cheese.

Keep salad dressings simple with these foundational formulas:

- 3 parts oil : 1 part vinegar

- 3 parts oil : 1 part lemon juice

- 2 parts olive oil : 1 part yogurt

- Olive oil, lemon juice, salt and pepper

- Olive oil, balsamic or red wine vinegar, Dijon mustard

Beyond vinaigrettes, dress salads with fresh lemon or lime juice and a drizzle of olive oil. Rubbed raw garlic and coarse salt make a bold topping. Pureed roasted red peppers or sun dried tomatoes blended with olive oil and herbs also make delicious dressings.

With fresh greens and vegetables, flavorful herbs, and simple homemade dressings, you can create an endless array of satisfying salads. Let seasonal produce guide your creations for Mediterranean flair.

Hearty Soups and Stews

Soups and stews are cornerstones of the Mediterranean diet, bringing vegetables, beans, whole grains and herbs together in cozy, nourishing one-pot meals. These dishes highlight seasonal produce and plant-based proteins for meals that comfort yet energize. While endlessly variable, Mediterranean-style soups and stews share common traits like rich flavor, texture, and ample nutrition.

In the Mediterranean region, soup is traditionally served as a first course to awaken the palate and prime the digestive system. Hearty bean or lentil soups provide protein and fiber absent from many Western diet starters like salad. Alternatively, gazpacho-style chilled raw vegetable soups provide hydration on hot days.

To make any vegetable soup Mediterranean-inspired, start with a base of aromatic alliums and herbs like onion, garlic, leeks and celery. Sauté these briefly in olive oil to develop depth. Tomato paste and spices like paprika or saffron lend sweetness and color.

Feature any seasonal vegetables by dicing or roasting chunks of carrots, parsnips, squash, zucchini, cauliflower, potatoes and dark leafy greens. Frozen produce works well too. Cook vegetables until just tender to retain nutrients.

Pulse portions of the soup to thicken it while leaving some chunks for body and texture. Alternatively, puree completely for a silky texture.

Beans such as chickpeas, white beans, or lentils add plant-based protein and satisfy hunger. Barley, farro or whole grain pasta make excellent additions too.

Nutrient-packed greens blend easily into soups. Chopped kale, escarole, spinach or chard wilt down for an injection of vitamins.

For added Mediterranean flavor, finish with fresh herbs like parsley, basil, oregano or mint. Ladle over croutons or bread. Lemon and Parmesan or feta cheese provide brightness.

Hearty bean or lentil stews also sustain energy with less meat than traditional Western versions. Start by sweating Mediterranean aromatics like peppers, onions and garlic in olive oil.

Sear chunks of eggplant, cauliflower, potatoes or squash to add heft and texture. Cook just until tender but not mushy.

Deglaze the pan with red wine or broth. Tomato products like chopped tomatoes, sauce or paste lend sweetness, color and nutrients.

Add cooked chickpeas, white beans, lentils or shelled edamame at the end to heat through. They will soften but maintain their shape.

Piquant spices like cumin, paprika, cinnamon and chile peppers add wonderful seasoning. Balance with cooling fresh herbs before serving.

While soups and stews can take some time to prepare, the hands-off simmering time gives opportunity for other tasks. Their nourishment lasts for multiple meals too.

Make extra portions to freeze, reheat and eat later in the week for effortless meals. Soup and stew also improve in flavor with a couple days in the refrigerator as spices meld.

For easy soup prep, save vegetable scraps like stalks, skins and ends in a bag in the freezer. When ready to cook, empty the veggie bag into a pot with aromatics and stock for practically free soup stock.

To save on chopping time, buy pre-diced frozen mirepoix or sofrito base mixes. Sweet potatoes and butternut squash also come pre-chopped frozen. Just sauté and simmer!

While traditional Mediterranean cuisine relies on whatever vegetables are fresh and abundant, don't be limited by season or region. Embrace produce from around the world to make soup your own.

Roast bones before making broth for deeper flavor. Braise meats like chicken thighs before adding to soup for ease. Use an electric pressure cooker to quickly cook dried beans from scratch.

Soup and stew are infinitely adaptable, so relax about adhering to strict recipes. Make them your own with whatever vegetables, whole grains, beans and seasonings you enjoy. These humble, hearty one-pot meals will become Mediterranean diet staples.

Sandwiches and Wraps with a Mediterranean Twist

Sandwiches and wraps make convenient, customizable Mediterranean diet lunches. Whole grain breads and wraps stuffed with fresh veggies, greens, lean proteins and flavorful spreads satisfy midday hunger in a healthy, portable meal.

Seek out whole-wheat pita, sourdough, rye or multi-grain loaves and flatbreads. Look for options with at least 3 grams of fiber per serving. Sprouted grain and Ezekiel breads provide nutty flavor and dense texture.

Boost nutrition by loading sandwiches up with vegetables. Spinach, arugula, mixed greens, tomato, cucumber, roasted peppers, sprouts, mushrooms and grated carrots all make delicious additions. Grilling or roasting veggies intensifies flavors.

Smear spreads like hummus, baba ghanoush or avocado directly on wraps or bread before piling on veggies. Olive oil, lemon juice, mustard and pesto also provide flavor. Go light on condiments like mayo, cheese or deli meats high in sodium.

Incorporate Mediterranean proteins like egg, tuna, Salmon, or chicken. Tuna salad with diced celery and light mayo tastes delicious on toast. Leftover salmon flakes beautifully in wraps with dill and greens.

Switch up ordinary sandwiches with flavors like sun dried tomato pesto, tapenade, feta cheese, basil, mint, roasted garlic or chimichurri sauce. Intensifying taste prevents boredom.

Try new sandwich and wrap combinations to discover favorites, for example:

- Chicken, avocado, tomato, arugula, hummus, sprouts on whole grain

- Tuna mixed with lemon and olive oil on greens in whole wheat pita

- Egg salad with scallions and mustard on rye toast

- Roasted vegetables, feta, pesto in spinach wrap

- Leftover salmon, dill, tomato, cucumbers and Greek yogurt sauce

Pack sandwiches and wraps for work or school in reusable containers rather than disposable plastic bags. An insulated bag with ice packs keeps items cool.

Slice sandwiches and wraps into smaller portions you can eat one handed. Bite sized pieces prevent fillings from falling out so you can enjoy on the go.

Swap chips or cookies for healthy sandwich companions like veggie sticks, fresh fruit, nuts, seeds or air popped popcorn. A piece of dark chocolate makes a satisfying treat.

Whip up a big batch of sandwich or wrap fillings on your day off to build easy lunches all week long. Store seasoned proteins, veggies, spreads and sauces in individual containers ready to assemble.

Whether enjoyed at your desk or al fresco, Mediterranean-style sandwiches and wraps make lunch a portable and pleasurable way to energize your afternoon.

Seafood and Plant-Based Options

The Mediterranean diet emphasizes seafood, plant-based proteins, and smaller amounts of poultry and red meat. This provides health benefits compared to meat-centric Western diets. This chapter explores how to incorporate more seafood and plant proteins into your routine for Mediterranean flair. You'll find tips for buying and preparing fish along with plant-based recipe ideas.

Eating ample seafood, especially fatty fish like salmon, delivers anti-inflammatory omega-3 fatty acids. Clams, mussels, oysters and squid also supply key nutrients. Keep canned tuna on hand for quick meals and snacks. Seek out sustainable, low mercury options when possible.

Select fresh seafood the day you plan to cook it. Look for glistening, firmly fleshed fillets without strong odors. If buying frozen, choose plain fillets rather than battered options. Thaw in the fridge overnight before cooking. Roast, grill, pan sear or bake fish using simple seasonings like lemon, herbs and olive oil to allow the delicate flavor to shine.

Beans, lentils and soy foods like tofu, tempeh and edamame offer plant-based protein. They supply satiating fiber to keep you feeling fuller longer. Canned beans make quick additions to soups, salads, grain bowls and stews. Swap half the ground meat in recipes like chili or meatballs for lentils or beans to boost nutrition.

Get creative with tofu by pressing, draining and marinating it, then sautéeing or roasting until golden. Blend silken tofu into smoothies. Soy curls soaked in broth make a remarkably meaty taco or stir fry filling. Textured vegetable protein (TVP) adds lean protein to pasta sauces, soups and chilis.

When preparing plant-based meals, think beyond just removing the meat. Layer in complex flavors with spices like cumin, paprika, curry and harissa. Cook with umami-rich ingredients like mushrooms, tomatoes, miso paste and nutritional yeast. Add texture with nuts, seeds and roasted vegetables.

Here are some recipe ideas to expand your seafood and plant-based Mediterranean options:

- Pan roasted salmon with dill yogurt sauce

- Sheet pan cod with cherry tomatoes, potatoes

- Curried chickpea stew over brown rice

- Black bean and veggie tacos with salsa

- Walnut lentil meatballs with marinara

- Grilled eggplant rollatini with tofu ricotta

- Chickpea tuna salad sandwiches

Varying your protein sources improves nutrition while keeping meals exciting. Let the healthy cultures of the Mediterranean guide you in exploring more seafood, beans, lentils and plant-based dishes.

Tips for Packing Healthy Lunches

Packing nutritious and satisfying lunches is key to stick with the Mediterranean diet amid busy workdays. Thoughtfully planned meals prevent the temptation of grabbing unhealthful takeout or vending machine options. Filling your lunchbox with Mediterranean staples also saves money compared to dining out. With smart prep and storage strategies, assembling tasty portable lunches is totally doable.

Make a little extra at dinner to repurpose leftovers into lunch. Grain bowls, hearty salads, roasted vegetables, or proteins readily transform into lunches with minimal effort. Store components separately then assemble the night before.

Get into the habit of making double batches when cooking grains, beans or proteins. Having pre-cooked ingredients ready to go streamlines lunch packing. Stock your fridge with roasted veggies, boiled eggs, cooked chicken and prepared hummus.

Wake up early enough to allow some morning prep time if needed. Tasks like scrambling eggs, toasting nuts or packing a salad take just a few minutes with practice. Set out containers and ingredients the night before for smoother mornings.

When grocery shopping, choose items with lunch meals in mind. Buy portable produce like cherry tomatoes, carrots sticks, snap peas, apples, oranges, bananas, and diced melons.

Seek snacks that multitask as mini-meals, like yogurt, cottage cheese, hard-boiled eggs, tuna pouches, nut butters with apples, and hummus with veggies. Healthy fats and protein boost satiation.

Make a big batch of whole grains like brown rice, farro, quinoa or barley on your day off. Portion these out for quick grain bowls later on. Hearty whole grain salads work well too.

Get creative with sandwiches by using Mediterranean style flatbreads, rolls, or wraps instead of regular bread. Fill them with roasted vegetables, greens, avocado, hardboiled eggs, canned fish or beans.

Take salad up a notch by using hearty grains as the base instead of lettuce. Top mixed grains with chickpeas, lentils, beans, nuts, seeds, and vinaigrette rather than creamy dressing.

Mix and match Mediterranean proteins throughout the week - try canned fish like salmon or tuna, sliced turkey, hard boiled eggs, or plant-based options like edamame and beans.

Make cold pasta or grain salads more satisfying by adding hemp seeds, mixed greens, artichoke hearts, olives, roasted veggies, beans, or shredded chicken.

Keep washed and chopped produce in containers to conveniently toss together quick Mediterranean salads full of cucumbers, bell peppers, carrots, olives, grape tomatoes, etc.

Blend or buy portable hummus, baba ghanoush, or Greek yogurt dip to pair with raw vegetables, toasted pita wedges, or whole grain crackers for instant snacks.

Make extra dinner soups, stews or chilis so leftovers can be packed as filling thermoses. Whole grains or cooked beans added to broths boost nutrition.

Prepare make-ahead Mason jar salads to grab from the fridge. Layer greens, grains or pasta, proteins, vegetables, herbs, nuts and dressing in a wide mouth jar.

Keep portable packages of unsalted nuts, seeds, and dried fruit to sprinkle atop meals for added energy, fiber and healthy fats.

Stash non-perishable snacks like whole grain crackers, roasted chickpeas, popcorn, dark chocolate, or homemade energy bites to supplement fresh foods when needed.

Use mini coolers with ice packs if packing dairy, fish, meat or other perishable items. Insulated, divided lunch bags also help regulate temperature.

Thoroughly wash reusable containers and replace any that are cracked, stained or smell funky. Let containers fully dry before use for food safety.

With Mediterranean diet staples on hand and some advance preparation, packing healthy, satisfying lunches for work or school becomes second nature. A little planning sets you up for success all day long.

CHAPTER 4

DINNER RECIPES

Quick and Healthy Weeknight Dinners

After a busy day, spending hours cooking an elaborate meal rarely seems appealing. Fortunately the Mediterranean diet offers endless options for nutritious dinners that come together quickly on hectic weeknights. With the right strategies, you can enjoy flavorful homemade meals without sacrificing convenience.

Plan ahead on weekends to prep ingredients so dinner comes together effortlessly. Chop veggies, cook whole grains, marinate proteins, whip up sauces and store components ready to combine on busy nights. Simple advance prep work speeds the process.

Keep your pantry, fridge and freezer stocked with Mediterranean diet staples like canned beans, whole grains, frozen veggies and precooked proteins. Relying on these ready-made items prevents last minute trips to the store.

Take advantage of handy appliances that streamline cooking. A slow cooker lets you assemble dishes in the morning that cook unattended for hours. Pressure cookers quickly transform tough cuts of meat into tender meals.

Choose naturally fast-cooking proteins like eggs, seafood, chicken thighs and ground meats. Salmon fillets, shrimp and cod cook in under 10 minutes. Marinated chicken needs only a quick turn in a hot skillet or roasting pan.

Pair these speedy proteins with bagged salad greens, prewashed veggies, canned beans and quick-cooking whole grains like couscous or quinoa. Frozen vegetables like spinach, peas and broccoli sauté up in just minutes.

One-pot or one-pan meals keep prep and cleanup minimal on busy nights. Try skillet recipes like whole grain pasta primavera, sausage and peppers, or shrimp fried rice.

Sheet pan meals with protein and vegetables require only a quick chop and roast in the oven. Casserole bakes layered with grains and veggies serve the whole family conveniently.

Take advantage of the microwave when possible. Reheat leftovers or precooked proteins and steam vegetables for fast side dishes with no pans to wash.

Enlist any helpers you can find! Kids old enough to safely handle knives can wash produce and chop ingredients under supervision.

Build your weeknight dinner repertoire with reliable recipes you can prepare efficiently. Over time, mastering quick Mediterranean meals means you always have go-to options.

Here are some fast and healthy Mediterranean diet dinners perfect for busy weeknights:

- Veggie omelets with cheese and salad

- Whole wheat pita pizzas with vegetables

- Tuna or salmon cakes with roasted broccoli

- Veggie fried rice with egg and cashews

- Sheet pan chicken fajitas or kebabs

- Pasta with olive oil, garlic, tuna and capers

- Burgers on whole grain buns with oven fries

With the right tools, ingredients and strategies, you can enjoy Mediterranean deliciousness any night of the week without spending hours in the kitchen. Don't sacrifice health for convenience!

Delicious and Nutritious Seafood Dishes

The sparkling blue Mediterranean invites an abundance of fresh, flavorful seafood into local cuisines. Fish, shellfish and other fruits of the sea take center stage in many iconic Mediterranean dishes. Besides tasting incredible, seafood provides lean protein and heart-healthy omega-3 fatty acids. This chapter explores delicious ways to incorporate more seafood into your diet for optimal wellbeing. You'll find tips for cooking seafood perfectly along with Mediterranean-inspired recipes.

Seafood requires just a light hand to allow its delicate brininess to shine. Start with high-quality fresh or thawed frozen seafood. Pat dry before seasoning to help flavors adhere. Rub or marinate in olive oil, citrus, fresh herbs, garlic, mustard, spices, or wine before cooking. Roasting, grilling, sautéing, or poaching are all excellent preparations. Watch closely and don't overcook—opaque, flaky fish takes just 3-4 minutes per side for thin fillets. Shellfish and shrimp cook even quicker.

Aim for two or more servings of fatty fish like salmon, mackerel or sardines each week to get anti-inflammatory omega-3s. Enjoy white fish like cod, halibut or tilefish 1-2 times per week. Mix in mild shellfish like shrimp, clams and mussels. Anchovies add big flavor to pasta, pizza and salads. Canned tuna works nicely in salads, sandwiches or tossed with whole grains.

Here are some delicious Mediterranean seafood recipe ideas:

- Grilled salmon with zucchini, tomatoes, olives

- Sheet pan roasted cod with artichokes, lemon

- Cioppino stew with tomato broth, shrimp, mussels

- Linguine with clams in white wine garlic sauce

- Grilled swordfish skewers with chimichurri

- Tuna salad nicoise with green beans, potato

- Whole roasted fish with herbs and lemon

To round out seafood meals: serve with brown rice, quinoa, beans, lentils or whole grain pasta. Roast or grill seasonal vegetables like peppers, onions, tomatoes, zucchini or eggplant. Add marinated artichokes, roasted garlic, olives or spinach for Mediterranean flair. A crisp green salad or roasted vegetable side completes the plate.

The Mediterranean cultures have perfected cooking seafood to highlight its subtle briny sweetness. Follow their lead by sourcing excellent fish and shellfish and letting quality ingredients shine with simple preparations and herbs. Soon these nourishing seafood dishes will become weekly staples for health.

Grilled Vegetables and Legume-Based Recipes

Charring vegetables on the grill adds wonderful smoky depth while retaining nutrients compared to frying. Grilling fruits, vegetables, and skewers makes for fast, fun meals with minimal cleanup. Take advantage of summer's bounty with these Mediterranean-inspired grilled produce dishes:

Slice eggplant, zucchini, bell peppers, tomatoes, onions, peaches or nectarines intothick planks. Brush with olive oil and grill until softened with nice grill marks. Eat as is, chop into a salad, or layer into sandwiches or flatbread pizzas.

Make easy grilled veggie packets. Place chopped summer squash, bell peppers, onions, tomatoes, and mushrooms into a foil packet. Drizzle with olive oil, add herbs and seasonings, then seal and grill.

Grill wedges of romaine lettuce leaves until lightly charred. Drizzle with olive oil and lemon juice for a smoky Caesar salad. Add grilled salmon or chicken if desired.

Assemble colorful skewers with cherry tomatoes, mushrooms, zucchini, bell peppers, pineapple, peaches, halloumi cheese or tempeh. Brush with oil and acid for a fast grilled meal.

Char half lemons or limes cut side down. Squeeze over grilled vegetables, seafood, chicken or salads for smoky citrus flavor.

Brush portobello mushroom caps with olive oil and grill until tender. Stuff with garlicky spinach, roasted peppers, artichokes and feta for Mediterranean mushroom boats.

Grill thick bread slices brushed with olive oil for quick garlic bread. Rub raw garlic clove over one side before grilling for extra flavor.

Make veggie fajitas with slices of zucchini, bell pepper, onion, mushrooms, and pineapple. Serve in warmed whole grain tortillas with beans, salsa, guacamole, and herbs.

Score whole heads of cauliflower and Romanesco, then grill until charred and tender. Drizzle with tahini lemon dressing for showstopping side dishes.

Assemble kebabs with chunks of eggplant, zucchini, cherry tomatoes, mushrooms, bell pepper, halloumi cheese, shrimp or chicken. Brush with chimichurri sauce.

Grill wedges of watermelon, pineapple, nectarines, plums or peaches for caramelized fruit desserts. Drizzle with honey or serve over Greek yogurt.

Fire up vegetable-focused main dishes by pairing with protein-packed legumes like lentils, beans and chickpeas:

Cook dried beans from scratch. Soak overnight, drain, and simmer in broth until tender before grilling. Canned beans work too but may dry out.

Toss chickpeas or cannellini beans with olive oil, herbs and spices. Grill in a mesh basket, stirring frequently, until crisped and charred in spots. Sprinkle over salads, grain bowls and tacos.

Make lentil burgers by forming cooked lentils into patties with binds like mashed beans, egg, or breadcrumbs. Grill until heated through and slightly crisped.

Top flatbread pizzas with grilled veggies, legumes like white beans, and fresh mozzarella or feta for fast Mediterranean meals with less meat.

Grill eggplant and zucchini planks until tender and charred. Layer over mixed greens with warm lentils, roasted peppers, olives, hummus and vinaigrette.

Assemble grilled vegetable tacos or burrito bowls with cooked black beans or pinto beans, avocado, salsa and queso fresco or feta.

The sidewalk's your kitchen when grilling produce, legumes and more. Tailor kebabs, packets, burgers and meatless mains to use seasonal veggies and pantry staples for meals that sizzle.

Poultry and Meat Dishes, Mediterranean Style

While the Mediterranean diet emphasizes mostly plants, lean proteins like poultry, lamb and beef still make flavorful appearances. Taking care to choose quality cuts and prepare them thoughtfully retains their deliciousness while keeping portions moderate.

Select the leanest poultry and meat cuts available, ideally from pasture-raised or organic sources. Skinless chicken breasts, turkey cutlets and 95% lean ground meats offer healthier options. Don't shy away from flavorful dark poultry meat which contains more vitamins than white meat.

Trim visible fat and remove poultry skin before cooking to cut calories and saturated fat while retaining juiciness. Marinating lean meats in oil, citrus, herbs and spices keeps them moist when cooking.

Cooking method strongly impacts healthfulness. Grilling, broiling, roasting, sautéing, stir frying or cooking in a skillet allows fats to drain away rather than stewing or deep frying which causes them to be reabsorbed.

Portion sizes matter too. Limit meat to a palm sized serving or about 3 ounces, roughly the size of a deck of cards. Bulk up meals with hefty portions of vegetables, whole grains and beans.

Incorporate Mediterranean flavors to keep poultry and meat dishes interesting. A simple marinade of olive oil, garlic, lemon and oregano adds big flavor. Smoked paprika, cumin and cayenne lend a Spanish flair.

Here are some delicious ways to prepare poultry and meat for the Mediterranean diet:

- Chicken breasts roasted with lemon, olives, capers and rosemary

- Turkey cutlets sautéed in olive oil with fresh salsa

- Grilled lamb chops with tzatziki mint yogurt sauce

- Sirloin steak rubbed with garlic, thyme and black pepper

- Zucchini stuffed with lean ground beef, tomatoes, feta

- Pork tenderloin with fig glaze and roasted Brussels sprouts

Use small amounts of flavorful meats to enhance vegetable dishes. Chickpeas simmered in tomatoes gain depth with crumbled sausage. Massaged kale salad tops a pizza with a sprinkling of pepperoni.

Stretch ground meats further with additions like chopped mushrooms, lentils or oats. For dishes like meatballs, a 50/50 mix of meat and filler bulks up servings with less saturated fat.

Turn meat into a garnish rather than the main attraction in meals like grain bowls and flatbread pizzas by using smaller pieces. Flank steak fajitas need only thin slices atop heaps of veggies.

Whip up a big batch of seasoned meat, like grilled chicken breast strips, on the weekend to sprinkle into Mediterranean diet salads, soups, pastas and more all week long.

With thoughtful choices and preparation methods, even modest amounts of poultry and meat can add delicious depth to the Mediterranean diet without compromising health.

Family-Friendly Mediterranean Dishes

The Mediterranean diet offers a balanced way of eating that benefits the whole family. Its focus on fresh, minimally processed foods sets kids up for lifelong healthy habits while providing great flavor and variety. This chapter explores kid-friendly dishes and strategies for getting children excited about Mediterranean cuisine. You'll find tips for getting little ones involved in the kitchen along with recipes suited for pleasing both children and adults.

Kids are more likely to try new foods if they help select and prepare them. Bring children grocery shopping and let them pick out colorful produce like cherry tomatoes or cucumbers. At home, have them wash fruits and vegetables before meal prep. Give appropriate knife skills and kitchen tasks based on age like stirring, mashing beans, tearing lettuce or assembling kebabs on skewers.

Present new ingredients to children multiple times. It can take over a dozen exposures for kids to accept some foods. Offer just a small taste at first along with familiar foods. Find creative ways to incorporate vegetables into meals, like grating into meatballs or baking into frittatas.

Cut foods into fun shapes with cookie cutters or have kids help assemble rainbow-colored salad ingredients or pizza toppings on individual plates. Theme nights like taco Tuesdays or breakfast for dinner make mealtimes more playful.

Here are some Mediterranean-inspired recipes suited for family meals:

- Chicken kebabs with colorful bell peppers and pineapple

- Turkey meatballs with hidden zucchini and whole wheat breadcrumbs

- Vegetarian taco bar with beans, lettuce, tomato, cheese

- Mini whole wheat pitas with hummus, cucumber slices, olives

- Sheet pan salmon with roasted broccoli and potatoes

- Chickpea cookie dough energy bites with oats, sunflower seeds

- Spinach and cheese manicotti with marinara sauce

- Whole grain waffles topped with bananas and peanut butter

The Mediterranean diet provides an optimal foundation for kids' nutrition and development. Make meals and snacks kid-friendly by involving children in prep and highlighting colorful ingredients. With playfulness and patience, whole foods and adventurous eating will become a natural part of family life.

CHAPTER 5

SNACK AND DESSERT RECIPES

Healthy Mediterranean Snacks for On-the-Go

Snacking smart is key to lasting success on the Mediterranean diet. Nutritious snacks curb hunger between meals, boost energy and help manage cravings. Luckily, this eating style brims with grab-and-go snack options to fill you up whether at home, work, school or on the go.

For convenience, prep a week's worth of snacks on less busy days. Portion nuts into reusable containers or bags. Wash and chop veggies and fruits so they're ready to eat. Whip up homemade trail mixes and energy bites.

Pack non-perishable snacks like roasted chickpeas, unsalted nuts, popcorn, dark chocolate, whole grain crackers or fruit and nut bars in your purse, desk or car so healthy options are always on hand.

Pair carbohydrates with protein, fiber or healthy fat to stabilize blood sugar and increase satiety. Apple slices with peanut or almond butter, whole grain crackers with hummus, and Greek yogurt with berries make balanced snacks.

Fiber-rich fruit and vegetables are portable Mediterranean diet staples. Keep fruits like apples, bananas, grapes, oranges and pears on hand for quick energy. Baby carrots, snap peas, bell pepper strips and broccoli florets also travel well.

For fresh snack veggies on busy days, pick up precut options like carrot sticks, cauliflower florets, snap peas and broccoli at grocery store salad bars.

Dried fruits like apricots, dates, figs, raisins and cherries offer concentrated sweetness in small packages. Opt for no-sugar-added versions and watch portions to keep calories in check.

Trail mix makes an energizing snack you can customize with unsalted nuts and seeds, dried fruit, toasted coconut, cacao nibs and popped popcorn or whole grain cereal.

Blend or buy portable hummus, tzatziki or baba ghanoush for dipping raw vegetables like carrot and celery sticks, bell pepper strips, broccoli and cauliflower. Whole grain pita wedges work too.

Pack yogurt, cottage cheese, ricotta or hard boiled eggs for an easy protein lift. Sprinkle nuts, seeds or fresh fruit on yogurt or cottage cheese for extra nutrition.

Keep single-serve nut butters, guacamole, canned fish or tuna salad packs on hand to spread on whole grain crackers, pita chips, rice cakes or sliced apples.

Make chia pudding using chia seeds, milk and fruit that thickens overnight in the fridge for grab-and-go morning nourishment. Add nut butter for more protein.

Take popcorn beyond the microwave with stove popped kernels tossed in olive oil and spices like cumin, paprika, garlic powder or cayenne pepper.

Homemade no-bake energy bites, bars, oat muffins and banana breads make healthy, filling snacks with whole grains, nuts, seeds, and dried fruits.

Roast or air fry chickpeas seasoned with Mediterranean spices for crunchy high-protein snacks. Roasted edamame, tofu or soy nuts offer more protein-packed options.

Slice vegetables like cucumbers, bell peppers, carrots and celery, then pack with hummus or olive oil bean dip for portable crunchy vessels to scoop and dip.

With smart advance preparation, snack time on the Mediterranean diet can be full of vegetables, fruit, nuts, seeds, legumes and whole grains to keep you feeling satisfied all day.

Delicious Fruit-Based Desserts

Sweet fruit makes the perfect satisfying finale for Mediterranean meals. With nature's candy, you can create luscious desserts that satisfy sweet cravings in a more nutritious and wholesome way.

Take advantage of peak ripeness and seasonality with desserts highlighting fresh fruit. Berries, stone fruits, melons, citrus, pomegranates and tropical varieties all shine when allowed to fully ripen before harvesting.

Shop at local farmers markets or orchards during summer and fall to source the best local fruit packed with sun-kissed sweetness. Freezing lets you make the most of seasonal bounty year-round.

Preparing fruit simply to highlight its natural flavors takes little time. A fruit salad tossed with fresh mint and squeeze of citrus makes a light dessert. Blend frozen bananas with cocoa powder for dairy-free "ice cream."

Roasting fruits like pears, peaches, plums and figs coaxes out their inherent sweetness through caramelization. Their texture softens while flavors intensify.

Grilling stone fruits or pineapple adds delicious smoky char. The high heat caramelizes natural sugars to concentrated deliciousness. Grilled fruit jazzes up yogurt or ice cream.

Simmering fruit in a bit of water or wine along with spices like cinnamon, cardamom, ginger or star anise creates a quick compote. Chill and top with a dollop of yogurt.

Blending up smoothie bowls makes enjoying a big serving of fruit fun. Swirl in yogurt or milk for creaminess and top with nuts, seeds or coconut.

Make popsicles by pureeing fruit and freezing in molds. Kids of all ages enjoy them as cooler treats. Mix in chia seeds, nut milks or banana for creaminess.

Wake up to fruit by making ahead overnight oats in mason jars layered with chia seeds, milk and berries. The oats soften and flavors meld overnight.

Grill or broil fruits like pineapple, mango, apples or pears for delicious salsas to top Greek yogurt, ice cream or pancakes with a savory twist.

Preserve summer fruit at its best by making fresh jam. Cook berries gently with a bit of sugar, lemon and spices like cinnamon until thickened.

Whether you crave crunch, creaminess, warmth or chill, fruit forms the delicious, nourishing foundation for Mediterranean desserts. Mother Nature provides the perfect package of sweetness and nutrition.

Nut and Seed Snack Recipes

Nuts and seeds are nutritional powerhouses in the Mediterranean diet. Packed with protein, healthy fats, vitamins and minerals, they make satisfying snacks and additions to meals. This chapter explores creative ways to enjoy more nuts, seeds and nut butters while following a Mediterranean lifestyle. You'll find recipes for energy-boosting snacks, along with tips for soaking, roasting and flavoring nuts and seeds.

Tree nuts like almonds, walnuts, pistachios, pine nuts and pecans provide plant-based protein and anti-inflammatory fats. Nutritionally-dense seeds include chia, flax, hemp, pumpkin and sunflower. Nut and seed butters like almond butter and tahini (sesame seed butter) are Mediterranean diet staples.

Soaking nuts and seeds boosts their nutrition by removing enzyme inhibitors. Place in a bowl of filtered water for 8-12 hours before draining and roasting. To roast, spread on a baking sheet and bake 8-12 minutes at 350°F, tossing once. Add a pinch of sea salt, chili powder or other spices after roasting.

Make your own trail mix with roasted nuts, seeds and just a touch of dried fruit. Try pairing toasted pecans, almonds and walnuts with unsweetened coconut flakes, pumpkin seeds, dried cherries and apricots. Homemade granola bars or energy balls offer grab-and-go Mediterranean snack options.

Here are some nutritious Mediterranean snack recipes:

- Apple slices with almond butter

- Roasted chickpea snack mix with sunflower seeds

- Greek yogurt berry parfait with chia seeds

- Pistachio chocolate energy bites

- Pumpkin seed tzatziki with pita chips or veggies

- Tahini and herb stuffed dates

- Walnut spinach pesto with whole grain crackers

- Curried cashew trail mix with raisins

A handful of unsalted nuts or seeds satisfies crunchy cravings and provides sustaining protein and healthy fats. Nut and seed butters spread on apple slices or whole grain toast make complete snacks too. Simply crafted Mediterranean-style trail mixes, granola and energy balls will become grab-and-go favorites.

Dark Chocolate Delights

While the Mediterranean diet emphasizes whole, minimally processed foods, dark chocolate can be enjoyed in moderation as an occasional treat. Made from cacao beans, authentic dark chocolate provides antioxidants, iron, fiber and magnesium. Containing less sugar than milk chocolate, dark chocolate makes a more nutrient-dense choice. Here are tips for purchasing, savoring, and using dark chocolate:

Choose dark chocolate with at least 70% cacao for maximum benefits and less sugar. The higher the cacao percentage, the more intense the chocolate flavor. Start around 70% and work upwards as taste preferences adapt.

Avoid diluting benefits by limiting ingredients beyond cacao beans, cocoa butter, sugar and emulsifiers like soy lecithin. Milk, corn syrup and excessive cocoa butter are signs of overly processed products.

Scan labels and select chocolate with short ingredient lists,Free of artificial colors, flavors, preservatives and additives.

Fair trade and single origin bars support ethical, sustainable cacao farming. These attributes don't affect nutrition but do impact cacao producers.

Higher percentage chocolate has a more bitter, intense flavor. Balance bitterness by pairing with nuts, fruit or sea salt. Develop an appreciation for deep chocolate taste.

Portion chocolate thoughtfully, savoring just 1–2 small squares. Allow the chocolate to slowly melt in your mouth. Mindful eating prevents overconsumption.

Substitute chocolate with at least 85% cacao for up to half the sugar in baked goods like muffins, cookies and cakes. Adjust other liquids to balance the dryness.

Add a square or two of dark chocolate to smoothies or melted into homemade nut milk for flavor and antioxidants. Start with small amounts until adapted to bitterness.

To make chocolate bark, temper chocolate, spread onto a parchment lined baking sheet, then sprinkle with nuts, seeds, dried fruit, spices, coconut, or coffee grounds before cooling.

Blend avocado with cacao powder and sweeteners for creamy chocolate pudding full of antioxidants and healthy fats. Top with berries, nuts or shredded coconut.

Melt chocolate with a bit of plant-based milk or cream to make homemade ganache for drizzling over fresh fruit like bananas or strawberries.

Make chocolate energy or protein bites by mixing dark chocolate with sticky dates, nut butter, protein powder, oats and seeds. Roll into balls and refrigerate until firm.

Drizzle melted chocolate over popsicles made from blended banana and nut milk or coconut milk yogurt for a frozen chocolate covered treat.

Prepare chocolate chia pudding by mixing cacao powder into chia seeds soaked overnight in plant milk. Add sweetener if desired. Top with fruit before eating.

To make chocolate bark, temper chocolate, spread onto parchment paper, sprinkle with nuts, seeds, dried fruit or sea salt, and cool until set before breaking into pieces.

Shave or grate chocolate over oatmeal, yogurt, fruit, or roasted sweet potatoes for an easy flavor and antioxidant boost.

Enjoy a square alongside coffee or tea as many Mediterranean cultures do. Or sip rich hot chocolate made from warmed plant milk blended with cacao powder and honey.

The antioxidants and unique flavor of minimally sweetened dark chocolate make it a worthy occasional treat. Savor its rich essence as part of the Mediterranean lifestyle.

Healthy Beverage Options

Beverages provide essential hydration, yet sugary drinks undermine the diet's nutrition. The Mediterranean approach emphasizes quenching thirst with ample water, nutritious infused waters, coffee and tea. Limiting sweetened beverages helps sustain energy and waistlines.

Water forms the cornerstone, ideal for quenching thirst any time of day. Sparkling water provides a fizzy treat. Consuming adequate water supports metabolism, energy and health. Add lemon, lime, cucumber or berries to infuse subtle flavor.

While the Mediterranean diet includes moderate wine intake, limit alcohol to no more than one glass per day for women and two for men. Alcohol's calories reduce weight loss so imbibe carefully.

Coffee and tea shine with antioxidants and anti-inflammatory benefits. The Mediterranean diet encourages enjoying them in moderation without added sweeteners. Alternate with herbal teas like chamomile, peppermint or hibiscus for variety.

For a special treat, warm up nut milks like almond or oat and blend with spices like cinnamon, cardamom or vanilla. Sweeten gently with a bit of maple syrup or honey if desired.

If you indulge in sugary sodas or fruit drinks, gradually reduce their frequency to avoid excess calories. Flavor seltzer or mineral water with citrus wedges or diced fruit for tangy refreshment.

Stay hydrated before, during and after exercise with cool water. For intense or endurance exercise lasting over an hour, a sports drink or coconut water replenishes electrolytes lost through sweat.

When drinking alcohol, alternate each alcoholic beverage with a glass of water to stay hydrated and avoid overconsumption. Stop drinking alcohol 2-3 hours before bed to preserve sleep quality.

If drinking juice, stick to small 4-6 ounce portions of 100% fruit juices without added sweeteners. Whole fruits provide more filling fiber. Dilute juice with water or seltzer to cut sweetness.

Smoothies using milk or yogurt plus whole fruits provide nutrition, but easy to overconsume. Keep portions in check by splitting smoothies into two servings or diluting with ice and water.

Quench thirst first before considering calories. Drink water freely throughout the day. Beverages deliver refreshment, so carefully limit empty calories from mixers, juices or soda.

Here are some delicious and nourishing Mediterranean diet drink ideas:

- Water with lemon, lime, cucumber or watermelon

- Black, green or herbal tea unsweetened

- Coffee with a splash of milk or foamed milk

- Sparkling water with a squeeze of citrus

- Coconut water after exercise to replenish electrolytes

- Wine spritzer – wine diluted with sparkling water

- Smoothies using whole fruits and yogurt or milk

- Hot almond milk simmered with cinnamon and cardamom

Staying hydrated is essential, but be mindful of excess calories in beverages that undermine the Mediterranean diet's health benefits. Sip wisely and slake thirst with water.

CHAPTER 6

28-DAY MEAL PLAN

Week 1: Easing into the Mediterranean Diet

The first week focuses on making simple substitutions to start transitioning your eating habits.

Day 1:

- Breakfast: Greek yogurt with berries and almonds

- Lunch: Tomato soup with whole grain crackers

- Dinner: Veggie omelet with side salad

- Snack: Carrots and hummus

Day 2:

- Breakfast: Oatmeal with walnuts and cinnamon

- Lunch: Mediterranean tuna salad sandwich

- Dinner: Baked salmon with roasted potatoes and green beans

- Snack: Sliced apple with peanut butter

Day 3:

- Breakfast: Whole grain toast with mashed avocado

- Lunch: Lentil soup with whole grain baguette

- Dinner: Chicken kebabs with bell peppers and romaine salad

- Snack: Whole grain pita chips and tzatziki

Day 4:

- Breakfast: Veggie egg muffin

- Lunch: Greek salad pita wrap

- Dinner: Quinoa stuffed peppers

- Snack: Dates and walnuts

Day 5:

- Breakfast: Overnight oats with chia seeds

- Lunch: Hummus and veggie whole wheat wrap

- Dinner: Grilled shrimp skewers with brown rice and roasted broccoli

- Snack: Melon cubes with feta crumbles

Day 6:

- Breakfast: Nutty banana smoothie

- Lunch: Grilled chicken pita with cucumber and feta

- Dinner: Tuscan white bean soup with garlic bread

- Snack: Hardboiled egg and cherry tomatoes

Day 7:

- Breakfast: Veggie frittata

- Lunch: Tuna and white bean salad

- Dinner: Whole wheat pasta with lean bolognese

- Snack: Roasted chickpeas

Focus on making one recipe a day Mediterranean-inspired while keeping other meals simple. Substitute olive oil for other oils, introduce more veggies, eat fruit for dessert. Stay hydrated with water and herbal tea.

Week 2: Exploring New Flavors

This week plays with more authentic Mediterranean ingredients and dish ideas to awaken your palate.

Day 1:

- Breakfast: Shakshuka - poached eggs in tomato sauce

- Lunch: Mediterranean chopped salad with chickpeas

- Dinner: Pan seared cod with sautéed spinach over pasta

- Snack: Baba ganoush and pita chips

Day 2:

- Breakfast: Whole grain waffle with ricotta and lemon zest

- Lunch: White bean and veggie soup

- Dinner: Chicken souvlaki with tzatziki sauce

- Snack: Roasted red pepper hummus with crackers

Day 3:

- Breakfast: Fruit and yogurt smoothie

- Lunch: Grilled eggplant and mozzarella panini

- Dinner: Zoodles with basil walnut pesto

- Snack: Marinated olives

Day 4:

- Breakfast: Veggie omelet with feta

- Lunch: Mediterranean quinoa salad

- Dinner: Harissa roasted salmon with tomatoes

- Snack: Toasted pita with nut butter

Day 5:

- Breakfast: Overnight oats with almond milk

- Lunch: Hearty lentil and kale soup

- Dinner: Grilled lamb kebabs

- Snack: Dark chocolate almond bites

Day 6:

- Breakfast: Savory oat bowl with chickpeas

- Lunch: Roasted beet and feta salad

- Dinner: Vegetarian moussaka

- Snack: Sliced pear with pecorino cheese

Day 7:

- Breakfast: Nutty granola with yogurt

- Lunch: Tuna and garbanzo bean salad

- Dinner: Sheet pan chicken with artichokes and oregano

- Snack: Pumpkin seed trail mix

Have fun with full-flavored ingredients like harissa, preserved lemons, fresh herbs, marinated veggies, nuts and seeds. Let signature Mediterranean flavors shine through.

Week 3: Mastering the Mediterranean Lifestyle

This week integrates the Mediterranean diet and lifestyle fully into your routine.

Day 1:

- Breakfast: Veggie frittata with side of melon

- Lunch: Grilled salmon salad

- Dinner: Chicken souvlaki with roasted veggies

- Snack: Roasted chickpeas

Day 2:

- Breakfast: Overnight chia oats

- Lunch: Lentil and veggie soup with whole grain bread

- Dinner: Spicy shrimp and garbanzo bean skillet

- Snack: Fresh figs and pecorino cheese

Day 3:

- Breakfast: Nutty fruit and yogurt smoothie

- Lunch: Grilled vegetable and hummus wrap

- Dinner: Baked cod with tomato relish and quinoa

- Snack: Walnut date energy ball

Day 4:

- Breakfast: Broccoli and scrambled egg pita

- Lunch: Mediterranean tuna salad over greens

- Dinner: Chicken gyros with tzatziki

- Snack: Apple slices with almond butter

Day 5:

- Breakfast: Savory oatmeal with spinach and egg

- Lunch: White bean and artichoke salad

- Dinner: Pistachio crusted salmon with roasted asparagus

- Snack: Smoked almonds

Day 6:

- Breakfast: Veggie frittata muffins

- Lunch: Mediterranean chopped salad

- Dinner: Grilled eggplant rollatini with quinoa

- Snack: Fresh figs with ricotta

Day 7:

- Breakfast: Baked oatmeal with raisins and walnuts

- Lunch: Marinated chickpea salad sandwich

- Dinner: Grilled lamb with ratatouille

- Snack: Dark chocolate espresso beans

Make movement like walking, hiking or swimming part of your routine. Savor leisurely meals with loved ones. Immerse yourself fully in the Mediterranean lifestyle.

Week 4: Embracing the Mediterranean Diet for Life

This week builds on your new Mediterranean habits so you can sustain this lifestyle long-term.

Day 1:

- Breakfast: Vegetable frittata and fruit

- Lunch: Spinach salad with chickpeas and feta

- Dinner: Lemon pepper cod with brown rice and asparagus

- Snack: Hummus and carrot sticks

Day 2:

- Breakfast: Greek yogurt with mixed berries

- Lunch: Quinoa tabbouleh salad

- Dinner: Chicken pasta with sun-dried tomatoes and artichokes

- Snack: Toasted walnuts and raisins

Day 3:

- Breakfast: Shakshuka with whole grain toast

- Lunch: Orzo pasta salad with olives and tuna

- Dinner: Rosemary pork tenderloin with roasted potatoes and carrots

- Snack: Pecorino romano and pear

Day 4:

- Breakfast: Avocado toast with sunny side egg

- Lunch: White bean soup with swiss chard

- Dinner: Grilled shrimp skewers with tomato salad

- Snack: Roasted pistachios

Day 5:

- Breakfast: Overnight oats with almond milk and cinnamon

- Lunch: Egg salad pita sandwich

- Dinner: Seared salmon with zucchini noodles and basil

- Snack: Greek yogurt with mixed berries

Day 6:

- Breakfast: Savory oatmeal with mushrooms and spinach

- Lunch: Falafel pita with hummus and veggies

- Dinner: Chicken tagine with couscous

- Snack: Melon cubes and feta cheese

Day 7:

- Breakfast: Vegetable frittata with side of fruit

- Lunch: Kale caesar salad with chickpeas

- Dinner: Beef kofta kebabs with cucumber yogurt sauce

- Snack: Sliced apple with almond butter

Make the key principles second nature: load up on fruits, veggies, whole grains, beans, nuts, seeds, herbs and olive oil. Limit red meat and processed foods. Exercise and relax. Embrace the Mediterranean lifestyle!

Reflection and Adjustment: Personalizing Your Meal Plan

Over the past 28 days, you've made tremendous strides in adopting a Mediterranean diet and lifestyle. Take some time now to reflect on your experience so far.

- What worked well for you? Which foods, meals and recipes did you enjoy the most?

- Were there any foods or habits that were more challenging to incorporate?

- How did the meal plan suit your routine, schedule, and preferences?

- Do you feel you have more energy, better digestion, or other benefits from eating this way?

- Is there anything you'd like to adjust moving forward to make this diet work better for your lifestyle?

Use these reflections to personalize the meal plan to your tastes and needs. Feel free to swap out recipes or ingredients from the past 4 weeks to ones that you find more appealing.

The Mediterranean diet is flexible - it's not about perfection, but progress. Focus on making steady improvements over time rather than drastic changes overnight. Be patient with yourself and celebrate each positive step forward.

If you had setbacks some days, get back on track the next day without judgement. This is a journey of discovering healthy habits you can sustain lifelong. With commitment and self-compassion, the Mediterranean diet will continue enhancing your wellbeing for years to come.

CHAPTER 7

MAINTAINING THE MEDITERRANEAN DIET LIFESTYLE

Tips for Eating Out and Social Events

Dining out and attending social gatherings are part of life. With the right strategies, you can navigate menus and party spreads while sticking to your Mediterranean diet goals. A little planning and creativity keeps you on track so you can have fun without derailing your progress.

When possible, choose restaurants offering Mediterranean fare focused on seafood, plant-based dishes, and fresh ingredients. Lebanese, Greek, Spanish tapas and Italian spots often have tempting options.

Scope out menus online beforehand and identify dishes that align with the diet. Choose grilled, roasted or steamed proteins, vegetable sides, salads, and fresh seafood while limiting cheese, creamy sauces, and fried foods.

Ask how dishes are prepared and request modifications as needed to make them healthier. Opt for steamed or sautéed instead of fried. Hold butter, cheese or heavy sauces. Substitute veggies for starchy sides.

Order sampler platters or tapas-style to enjoy smaller portions of a variety of Mediterranean appetizers and sides like hummus, grilled vegetables, salads and fresh seafood.

Build a salad entree and load up with vegetables, chickpeas or lentils, walnuts, and avocado. Get dressing on the side to control the amount.

Select simply grilled, baked or broiled fish, seafood, chicken or lean meats. Pair with side salads and roasted, grilled or steamed market vegetables. Ask for extra lemon wedges.

Enjoy small portions of pasta in tomato-based or olive oil-based sauces. Request whole grain options if available or just eat a modest amount of regular pasta.

Split an entree with a dining partner to control portions of heavier dishes. Or box up half your meal to take home before digging in.

When dining at someone's home, offer to contribute a Mediterranean-friendly dish like vegetable soup, salad, grilled seafood, chicken or plant-based main to share.

Politely decline deep fried appetizers and heavy, creamy dips. Fill your plate with vegetable crudités, fresh fruit, mixed nuts, roasted chickpeas and other lighter options.

Focus on grilled, baked or roasted proteins and fill half your plate with vegetable sides. Decline seconds of starchy foods or rich desserts.

For potlucks and parties, prepare and bring Mediterranean-inspired foods like homemade hummus, olive tapenade, roasted vegetables, mixed nuts, grilled salmon, or a hearty bean or lentil dish.

Sip water with lemon between alcoholic drinks and limit consumption. Alcohol lowers inhibitions which can lead to poor food choices.

If you go off track, get right back on path at your next meal. Don't let one indulgence spiral into giving up your goals completely.

Keep healthy snacks like nuts, cut vegetables, jerky or an apple in your purse in case you get stuck hungry without good options.

Politely decline if urged to take home leftover heavy foods that don't align with your program. Recommend they save leftovers for other gatherings instead.

With practice navigating menus and party spreads, you can stick to the Mediterranean lifestyle while still enjoying social gatherings and dining out. Stay focused on fresh, wholesome foods.

Managing Cravings and Setbacks

Altering eating habits prompts challenging moments like cravings or setbacks. But with mindfulness and self-compassion, these become opportunities for growth. Be prepared to navigate temptations in a balanced way.

Cravings for sugary, fatty foods are normal, especially when first transitioning to the Mediterranean diet. Be curious about cravings instead of resisting them. What need might this craving represent?

Rather than banning certain foods, allow occasional small indulgences mindfully. Savor a few bites of chocolate slowly. Share a dessert with a friend. This prevents feeling deprived.

Wait out intense cravings 10-15 minutes to determine if acting on them aligns with your goals or not. Distract yourself by calling a friend, taking a walk or other activities.

Identify triggers like stress, boredom, or loneliness that tend to spark cravings. Develop new coping strategies when these emotions arise, like calling a friend or taking a bath.

Limit exposure to triggers. Avoid stocking sweets or junk food at home. Mute ads on social media promoting unhealthy items. Unfollow accounts glorifying foods that sabotage your goals.

Shifting habits prompts occasional setbacks like overindulging at a party or reverting to old ways when stressed. Expect these; change isn't linear. Reframe slip-ups as opportunities to identify triggers and build resilience.

Rather than harsh self-judgment after a setback, show yourself compassion. Talk to yourself as a trusted friend, with understanding. Criticism often backfires by spurring shame and abandonment of goals.

Get back on track with your next meal, not tomorrow or next week. Don't let a small stumble snowball into giving up entirely. Consistency compounds progress over time.

Reflect on what caused the setback and make a plan to handle that situation differently next time. Learning from challenges fosters lasting change.

Enlist social support. Share setbacks and cravings with a buddy. Talk through what happened without self-blame. Troubleshoot together how to navigate tricky situations in the future.

Celebrate non-scale victories like successfully managing a craving, meal prepping or choosing a healthy meal at a restaurant. Focus on achievements rather than perfection.

Cravings and setbacks are natural on the path to improved wellbeing. How you manage them determines long-term success. With self-compassion and resilience, they become stepping stones toward a healthier you.

Staying Motivated: Setting and Achieving Goals

Adopting any new eating pattern requires dedication, especially amid busy schedules and engrained habits. But staying motivated is possible with clearly defined goals, action plans, and systems that spur you onwards rather than relying on willpower alone. By applying evidence-based motivation strategies, your Mediterranean diet and lifestyle journey will unfold smoothly.

Start by getting clear on your "why." What sparked your interest in the Mediterranean diet originally? Improved health? Weight loss? More energy? Better lifestyle? Clarifying motivation provides direction and keeps you on track when challenges arise.

Set specific, measurable goals with deadlines, like eating 5 vegetable servings daily within 3 months. Having quantifiable aims focused on behaviors within your control is key. This also allows tracking progress.

But don't overhaul everything at once if that feels overwhelming. Modify goals to change one dietary habit every 2 weeks, like reducing sweets then boosting vegetables. Small steps build sustainable change.

Plan ahead for success by identifying potential barriers like busy schedules or cravings, and brainstorm solutions. This mental preparation prevents getting derailed by common obstacles.

Track behaviors like produce intake, single ingredient meals, exercise sessions, or other metrics. Monitoring progress is motivating and reveals what works versus potential improvements needed.

Pair new behaviors with existing habits to integrate them seamlessly into your routine. For instance, always eat a vegetable side with dinner or go for a walk before cooking supper.

Involve friends and family in your Mediterranean lifestyle for camaraderie, accountability and support. Cook, meal prep and be active together when possible. Share your journey.

Schedule Mediterranean cooking and physical activity into your calendar to make them priorities rather than afterthoughts. View them as appointments with yourself.

Curate a Mediterranean diet inspiration board with photos of ingredients, meals, travel destinations or activities. Visual cues reinforce motivation and intention.

Stock your kitchen and pantry with abundant fresh produce, whole grains, beans, lentils, nuts, seeds and healthy oils. Surround yourself with quick meal enablers.

Learn Mediterranean cooking skills by taking classes, following recipes and watching technique videos. Knowledge and ability help implement this way of eating.

When you feel motivation lagging, revisit your "why" or do a progress review. Pat yourself on the back for every goal met thus far. Small wins uplift.

Occasional indulgences or off days don't negate all your efforts. Get right back on track at the next meal instead of spiraling. Be kind to yourself.

Look beyond just weight to embrace holistic wellness goals like better sleep, balanced energy, improved skin or mental clarity. Benefits extend beyond the scale.

Infuse more joy and celebration into your relationship with food. Savor not just the health gains but also the flavors, scents, colors and community.

Replace old unhealthful emotional attachments to certain foods with new positive habits that uplift mood like walking, cooking and connecting with others.

Each small choice moves you along your path towards improved wellbeing. With preparation and patience, lasting motivation for the Mediterranean lifestyle will come from within.

Exercise and the Mediterranean Lifestyle

Physical activity powers the Mediterranean lifestyle's full-body benefits. Moderate movement energizes body and mind while controlling weight and reducing disease risk. Discover realistic ways to integrate enjoyable activities for improved wellbeing.

Aim for 150 minutes per week of moderate activity like brisk walking, swimming or cycling. Even shorter bursts of 25-30 minutes most days provide substantial benefits. Start where you are and build.

Incorporate strength training 2-3 times per week for overall fitness. Weight lifting, resistance bands, bodyweight exercises or yoga build muscle and bone density while increasing metabolism.

Focus on activities you enjoy rather than punishing workouts. Dancing, hiking, pickleball and gardening all get you moving. Playful recreation elicits powerful feel-good endorphins.

Integrate motion into everyday routines. Take the stairs, walk while on the phone, park farther away, stand when on public transit. Little bursts of activity add up.

Make exercise social to increase fun and consistency. Join a volleyball league, walking group or gym with friends. Scheduling fitness dates adds accountability.

Recruit family members for backyard games, evening walks or bike rides. Children enjoy moving together, setting good lifelong habits. Turn chores like yardwork into play.

If new to exercising, start gradually. Attempt too much initially increases soreness and injury risk. Build up duration and intensity over several weeks. Be patient with yourself.

Focus on feeling energized, capable and proud of showing up rather than speed, distance or calorie burn. Any activity has value.

Prevent boredom by mixing up your fitness routine. Alternate between walking, swimming and strength training. Take a Zumba class or hike a new trail periodically. Variety maintains motivation long-term.

Monitor intensity by ensuring you can maintain a conversation during workouts. If too winded to talk, dial it back to moderate exertion, ideal for health and calorie burn.

Stay hydrated before, during and after physical activity. Water is best for replenishment. Sports drinks containing electrolytes benefit high intensity exercisers.

Listen to your body. Rest when needed to allow muscles to recover and strengthen. Varying activity with rest days prevents overtraining.

The Mediterranean lifestyle sustainably improves fitness through joyful movement rather than punishing regimes. Discover activities you love doing and keep your body gently active most days of the week. Consistency and community deliver lasting results.

Long-Term Success: Making the Mediterranean Diet a Way of Life

The Mediterranean diet and lifestyle provide guidance not just for a few weeks or months, but for life. After an initial transition period, this way of eating becomes second nature rather than an imposed temporary diet. By embracing the Mediterranean diet as an enjoyable, lifelong eating pattern, you ensure ongoing nourishment, satisfaction and wellbeing.

Make gradual incremental changes rather than expecting perfection immediately. Small steps build more sustainable habits over time without getting overwhelmed.

Focus on adding in nourishing Mediterranean foods rather than restricting favorites. Abundance of produce, whole grains, beans, legumes, nuts and seafood crowds out less healthy choices.

Allow occasional indulgences in moderation without guilt. Deprivation leads to burnout. The Mediterranean diet is flexible - no food is totally off limits.

Listen to your body's signals. Eat when moderately hungry, stop when satisfied. Honor cravings with small portions of whatever is desired.

Cook meals at home as often as possible to control ingredients, portions and quality. Make cooking relaxing rather than a chore. Involve family and friends.

Meal prep staples like beans, grains, dressings and roasted vegetables on less busy days to use all week for fast Mediterranean meals.

Keep pantry and fridge stocked with key Mediterranean foods so healthy options are readily available - canned fish, beans, lentils, whole grains, nuts, seeds, herbs, spices, eggs, yogurt, etc.

Find your personal balance of tradition versus creativity. Blend classic Mediterranean dishes with globally inspired flavors reflecting your tastes and culture.

Adapt recipes to suit your dietary needs and restrictions. Substitute ingredients as required while retaining the spirit of the Mediterranean diet.

Seek variety within the eating pattern to prevent boredom - rotate seafood, legumes, whole grains, produce, herbs and spices.

Make substitutions rather than eliminations if giving up certain foods entirely feels impossibly daunting. For example olive oil instead of butter.

Discover physical activities you genuinely enjoy like walking, hiking, biking, swimming, dance or sports. Move in ways that feel good.

Incorporate movement and activity into daily routines - walk during lunch break, stretch while watching TV, take stairs, park farther away, etc.

Spend time outdoors as often as possible to recharge - garden, stroll through nature, have al fresco meals with loved ones.

Foster community through cooking, exercise and enjoying meals together. Share food and laughter around the table.

Practice mindfulness when eating by slowing down to savor flavors and textures. Appreciate the nourishment.

Focus on all that delicious Mediterranean foods add to your meals rather than what gets removed or restricted.

Be patient with yourself on the journey. Small missteps don't equate failure. Just resume the next healthy choice at your next meal.

The Mediterranean lifestyle adapts gracefully to cultures worldwide over generations because it focuses on joy, connection and celebration of wonderful fresh foods. Make this eating pattern your own for the long haul.

CONCLUSION

The Impact of the Mediterranean Diet on Your Life

Embracing the Mediterranean lifestyle yields profound holistic benefits surpassing improved health metrics. Adopting Mediterranean diet principles positively transforms not just your body but also emotional wellbeing, relationships, leisure time, and more.

As your nutrition improves, energy and mental clarity increase enabling greater productivity at work or school. Wholesome foods give the steady energy to tackle big projects or ace exams without crashes. Clear thinking fosters efficiency.

Making better food choices reduces risk for chronic diseases down the road. Knowing you are investing in lifelong vitality provides comfort and empowerment. Daily actions shape long-term health.

Savoring cooking and meals awakens your senses. The Mediterranean diet reconnects you to food's flavors, textures and aromas through home cooking and convivial dining.

Mealtimes become occasions for joyful connection. Sharing delicious Mediterranean meals brings loved ones together to unwind and talk. Food nourishes relationships.

More time enjoying home cooked meals means less reliance on takeout, drive-thrus and eating on the run. You gain free time no longer spent waiting in restaurant lines.

The flexibility of the Mediterranean diet prevents deprivation. Occasionally enjoying treats or restaurant meals in moderation keeps this lifestyle pleasurable rather than punishing.

Exploring new ingredients, cuisines and recipes makes cooking and eating fun adventures rather than monotonous chores. It feels creative, not restrictive.

As the Mediterranean diet becomes your new normal, keeping weight in check gets effortless. No more yo-yo dieting or deprivation. You simply feel and look your best.

Walking, gardening and other moderate physical activity weave into your days naturally with this lifestyle. Moving your body energizes and lifts your mood.

More activity and nourishing foods bolster your immune system, making you more resilient against colds, flu and infections. You bounce back faster when they occur.

Eating Mediterranean diet style becomes an act of self-care, valuing health and savoring life's pleasures. It feels nurturing, not punishing.

This fulfilling lifestyle lets you engage more fully in relationships, passions and goals. When you care for your whole self, you can show up for the people and activities you cherish.

The Mediterranean diet makes each day more enjoyable while optimizing wellbeing for years to come. Adopting this lifestyle rewards you with benefits surpassing a number on the scale.

Continuing Your Journey Towards Health

Embracing the Mediterranean lifestyle sets you on an ongoing path towards vibrant wellbeing. As the diet and active living habits become your new normal, you will continue reaping benefits for body and mind. This way of eating and moving provides guidance not just for a few weeks or months, but for life.

After an initial transition period, the Mediterranean diet's principles become ingrained. Shopping, cooking, and dining Mediterranean style feels effortless with practice. You learn how to adapt and customize this flexible approach to suit your needs.

While weight loss may occur in the beginning, the focus shifts to holistic health - abundant energy, balanced moods, restful sleep, longevity and retained mobility as you age.

Ongoing nourishment from diverse fresh foods high in antioxidants, healthy fats and fiber supports cell renewal and a strong immune system. Inflammation is kept in check.

As processed foods, sweets and excess salt, unhealthy fats and empty calories are gradually phased out, you feel more energetic and less lethargic after eating.

Persistent health conditions affected by diet and lifestyle may steadily improve through adherence to Mediterranean principles of whole foods and active living.

Joint health retains flexibility to continue regular activity thanks to anti-inflammatory omega-3 fats from seafood and oils, plus the lubricating benefits of staying active.

Risk of heart disease and stroke continues declining as blood pressure, cholesterol, triglycerides and circulation improve via the diet and physical activity.

With balanced nutrition and regular activity, your sleep normalizes and deepens for increased daytime productivity, improved mood and clearer thinking.

The social connections and sense of community fostered through cooking, dining and exercising together enriches quality of life and emotional health.

As seasonal produce dictates yearly rhythms, you feel more aligned to natural cycles through eating what is ripe and abundant.

The relaxed pleasurable approach to meals focused on quality, moderation and variety helps maintain a healthy relationship with food.

With knowledge of this lifestyle, you have tools to get back on track after occasional indulgences, vacations or busy periods rather than spiraling.

The act of preparing and enjoying wholesome Mediterranean meals becomes an opportunity to unwind, express creativity and care for yourself and loved ones.

You grow more attuned to your body, energy levels and moods, learning when you truly need rest versus when movement will uplift you.

Aging gracefully with strength, mobility and sharp faculties becomes possible thanks to ongoing nutritious eating and activity.

The kitchen grows into a hub for connection, laughter and nourishment shared with family and friends old and new.

You find renewal continuously through nature – gardening, outdoor movement, harvesting bounty from your own land or community green spaces.

This sustainable lifestyle gives you inner resources to cope with life's ups and downs through nourishing food, activity, community, nature and mindfulness.

The Mediterranean path has no end point; it evolves with you through life's phases, continually guiding you back to wellness.

The Role of Community in Sustaining Lifestyle Changes

Embracing the Mediterranean lifestyle long-term requires a supportive community. Surrounding yourself with those who uplift your efforts makes staying on track infinitely easier. Prioritize people who champion your goals.

Connect with like-minded people seeking health through Facebook groups, Meetups, or apps. Share tips, recipes and struggles with a virtual community adopting a similar lifestyle. Camaraderie gives motivation on tough days. You realize you aren't alone in challenges.

Recruit friends or family members to embark on this journey together. Changing habits as a group provides accountability through gentle peer pressure. You feel obligated to stay on track when others are counting on you.

Turn cooking and meals into fun social occasions rather than isolated chores. Invite friends over for Mediterranean potlucks. Grill pizzas on the patio together. Conversation makes prep time fly.

Involve family in menu planning, grocery shopping and cooking dinner together. Children gain lifelong healthy habits when eating wholesome foods becomes the new normal from a young age.

When dining out, suggest Mediterranean restaurants to make selecting healthy options easy. Seek dishes showcasing vegetables, whole grains and lean proteins. Herbivore friends will appreciate plant-based choices.

Politely communicate lifestyle changes to hosts when invited to social gatherings. Most will happily accommodate preferences. Offer to bring a healthy dish to share.

Surround yourself with positive people who applaud small wins like choosing a salad over fries or turning down dessert. Negativity sabotages self-esteem and resolve.

Let loved ones know the best way to support your efforts is avoiding judgment or criticism. You need champions, not critics questioning if these changes will last.

Find a workout buddy to make fitness more fun. Join a running group or take a healthy cooking class together. Social obligation helps consistency.

Share your Mediterranean lifestyle on social media. Posting meal preps, recipes and workouts encourages others while reinforcing your commitment through public declaration of goals.

When setbacks happen, confide in trusted friends for encouragement, not condemnation. Their empathy renews motivation to get back on track.

Implementing lasting positive changes succeeds best with a robust support network. Making health a social endeavor rather than solo quest amplifies your commitment and makes the Mediterranean diet deliciously sustainable.

BONUS 1

98 VIDEO TUTORIAL RECIPES

Scan the QR code

Thelma Ansen

BONUS 2

14 VIDEO TUTORIALS

Scan the QR code

BONUS 3

RECIPES IDEAS

Scan the QR code

EXCLUSIVE BONUS

3 EBOOK

Scan the QR code or click the link and access the bonuses

http://subscribepage.io/01tYl3

AUTHOR BIO

Thelma Ansen

Thelma Ansen is a talented writer in the field of cooking, known for her ability to share culinary knowledge in an accessible and engaging way. With an innate passion for food, Thelma has dedicated her life to exploring and experimenting with new recipes, ingredients, and techniques.

Her path to success began at a young age, when Thelma spent hours in the kitchen with her mother, learning the secrets of traditional dishes and developing a deep love for the culinary arts. After completing her studies in gastronomy, she began working in renowned restaurants, honing her skills and taking on increasingly complex culinary challenges.

However, Thelma soon felt the need to share her knowledge with a wider audience. Determined to make cooking accessible to all, she began writing one-of-a-kind cookbooks. Her ability to synthesize complex information in a simple and understandable way made her books an instant success.

Thelma's recipes range from traditional to innovative dishes, always with an eye toward health and wellness. She experiments with fresh, seasonal ingredients, encouraging readers to explore new flavors and follow a healthy, balanced lifestyle.

Printed in Great Britain
by Amazon

42212875R00059